Y0-ASP-034

HARTFORD PUBLIC LIBRARY

All in the First Family

ALL IN THE FIRST FAMILY

THE PRESIDENTS' KINFOLK

BILL ADLER
WITH NORMAN KING

G. P. PUTNAM'S SONS
NEW YORK

Copyright © 1982 by Bill Adler Books, Inc.
All rights reserved. This book, or parts thereof,
must not be reproduced in any form without permission.
Published simultaneously in Canada by
General Publishing Co. Limited, Toronto.

Library of Congress Cataloging in Publication Data

Adler, Bill,
    All in the first family.

    Includes index.
    1. Presidents—United States—Family—Anecdotes,
facetiae, satire, etc. I. Title.
E176.1.A43 1982   973   81-15827
ISBN 0-399-12682-1   AACR2

PRINTED IN THE UNITED STATES OF AMERICA

Contents

Preface by Ron Nessen		7
Introduction		9
1	My Son, My Son!	15
2	Big Brother Should Be Watching!	26
3	More Sad Bad Glad Mad Brothers	44
4	Am I My Sister's Keeper?	57
5	Rascals, Rapscallions, and Other Relations	73
6	Damsels in Distress	89
7	More Beautiful People	109
8	The Degeneration Gap	134
9	The Papas and the Mamas	168
10	Threesome at the Bar Sinister	191
11	Inlaws and Outlaws	206
12	Heroin, Homicide, and Horror	235

Preface

by Ron Nessen

You can choose your friends (and even your enemies) but, for better or worse, you're stuck with your relatives.

And nobody knows that better than the 39 presidents of the United States.

I mean, a president expects to be held accountable for his economic program and his foreign policy. But he can only look on in helpless bemusement—or embarrassment—when the newspapers and the TV news are filled with the latest imbroglio involving the First Lady, the First Children, the First Sibling, or the First Parent.

When Chief Executives are stuck with troublesome relatives, so are we. Voters who think they are voting only for a president, find out they get the whole family. And what a colorful, comical, corrupt, raffish, daffy, dippy, and just plain wacko bunch of First Families we have chosen!

Their stories are told in rich and fascinating detail—often

humorous, sometimes poignant—in this readable book of memorable anecdotes.

A president's character is molded to a large extent in the family. His temperament, his personality, his moods, his attitude toward his fellow humans, are all forged by the private pain and pleasure, by the foibles and support, by the very genes, of the First Family.

So, if you want to know our presidents, know their wives, their children, their parents, their brothers and sisters, their in-laws. It is a perspective that throws a telling light on American history.

Introduction

A drunkard and wastrel . . . an enemy spy . . . a suspected arsonist . . . a swindler and cheat . . . a philanderer and suicide . . . a committed lunatic . . . a jailbird and profligate . . . a drug addict . . . a murderess on trial. In spite of the various degrees of dissolution and depravity, all these people have one thing in common. Each is a member of America's First Families.

The drunkard and wastrel was Charles Adams, son of John Adams, the second president of the United States. The enemy spy was James A. Semple, son-in-law of John Tyler, the tenth president of the United States. The suspected arsonist was Jane Randolph Jefferson, mother of Thomas Jefferson, the third president of the United States. The swindler and cheat was Abel Rathbone Corbin, brother-in-law of Ulysses S. Grant, the eighteenth president of the United States. The philanderer and suicide was George Washington Adams, son of John Quincy Adams, the sixth president of the United States. The committed lunatic was Mary Todd Lincoln, First Lady of Abraham Lincoln, the sixteenth president of the United States. The jailbird and profligate was Payne Todd, stepson of James Madison, the fourth president of the United States. The drug addict was David Anthony Kennedy, nephew of John F. Kennedy, the thirty-fifth president of the United States. The murderess on trial was Anne Cary Randolph, cousin of Thomas Jefferson, the third president of the United States.

The First Family is America's version of royalty: a focus of national attention, inspiration, and tribute. A European royal family sports its rakes and its dissolutes; so does the First Family. There the similarity ends. European royalty is inbred and very homogenous in blood lines. The interest of the American First Family is its infinite variety. At its epicenter is the president of the United States, an unknown quantity—indeed, a question mark—from the moment he enters the White House to govern the nation. Every eye is focused on him but no one knows how he will react to power and pitfalls. He brings with him to share the focus for good or ill, a whole cast of characters—the First Family. And how will they act?

Most important is the First Lady. She may be inconspicuous, she may be charming, she may be ugly, she may be glamorous, or she may be practically invisible. She may be a Beautiful Person like Jacqueline Kennedy; a rugged frontierswoman like Rachel Jackson (who even though she never lived to enter the White House was undeniably a First Lady); or an energetic, high-strung, ambitious woman like Mary Lincoln. Whoever she is, she receives almost as much attention in the press and in public as the president himself.

Next in importance come the First Children. Some are large broods like the Roosevelts or the John Tylers—the latter fathered fourteen! Some have become famous in their own right, like First Son John Quincy Adams, who became president himself.

Next come the brothers and sisters of the president. Who could forget Billy Carter, First Brother to Jimmy Carter who became the Last Straw? Or Ruth Carter Stapleton, the faith healer who tried crashing into books before brother Jimmy even got to Washington?

Among conspicuous presidential parents was Nancy Hanks, Abe Lincoln's mother. She became a problem for biographers when they tried to discover whether or not she was illegitimate (she was). And Abigail Smith Adams, who was First Lady to one president (John Adams) and the mother of another (John Quincy Adams).

How does the president react when he discovers a skeleton in the closet? And how do members of the First Family respond to living in a goldfish bowl?

Maureen Reagan, daughter of President Ronald Reagan, put it simply: "I resent it."

First Families are subjected to such scrutiny and publicity that they begin to believe their own press notices. The focus of this book will be on those who became a risk to the administration; those who made foolish decisions that affected the president's judgment, and hence the fate of the nation.

All in the First Family

1
My Son, My Son!

"The kids never fitted into the public's image of what Ronald Reagan's children should be," an aide of President Reagan once said. "Everyone thought his children should be totally square and go by the books. But that didn't happen. They are not the Goody Two-shoes types."

Indeed not.

There are two sons and two daughters. Out of two male heirs, both gave pause to their father at one time or another, and caused some concern on their father's way to and sojourn inside the White House.

Michael Reagan is the oldest son. He was adopted when he was just four days old by Ronald Reagan and his first wife, actress Jane Wyman. They already had one girl, Maureen. By the time young Mike was four years old, the marriage was on the rocks, and Jane took their two children and went her own way.

When Reagan remarried he had two more children by Nancy Davis, whose name at birth was Nancy Robbins but was changed to conform to her stepfather's surname. The son and daughter of Ronald and Nancy's marriage are Ronald Prescott Reagan and Patricia Davis.

Ronald Prescott Reagan was not called Junior because his name differs from his father's, which is Ronald Wilson Reagan. Patti Davis changed her last name to conform to her mother's adopted name, because she didn't want to trade on her father's famous name when she started her career in show business.

The two sets of children did not grow up together in a normal family situation. Theirs was a stereotypic Hollywood double-marriage family milieu, with the kids getting together on weekends, if at all, and with most of the family living away from one another much of the time.

Besides that, there was no lasting affection between the two wives. "I don't think Nancy Reagan had any love for the Wyman kids," an associate of Reagan's once said. "I think she felt she would like to have any previous associations of Ronald's wiped out. She built a wall around him that the older kids couldn't break through."

It wasn't an easy life, growing up with an extremely famous and recognizable father. Mike didn't know either of his parents very well until he was an adult. His mother, Jane Wyman, was always out on a set shooting a movie.

"I saw mom only on weekends," he said. "I didn't get to know dad until I was twenty-five."

Mike and Maureen spent their formative years away at one school or another.

"The best place for us"— meaning for him and for Maureen—"was boarding school." He said it not to be sarcastic, but to impart a kind of truth about the life of a celebrity's offspring.

The truth of the matter was that Jane Wyman's career had begun to take off; Ronald Reagan's was in a slump. That disparity had a great deal to do with their splitup.

The same problem was not liable to come up with Reagan's

second wife, Nancy Davis, who also was an actress. In fact, Nancy Reagan quit show business forever once she married—and never looked back.

Nancy Davis had plenty of show business friends, through her actress-mother. Spencer Tracy, Walter Huston, and ZaSu Pitts, among others, helped her as much as they could. She left Broadway to sign a contract with MGM, and it was there, some six years later, that she met Ronald Reagan—and became a woman of the family rather than a woman of the stage and screen.

Possibly the different degrees of success in their stage careers had something to do with the stand-off attitude between Jane Wyman and Nancy Davis. Whatever caused it, it had an effect on the children of both women.

Mike Reagan, Jane's son, never seemed to be able to get it all together when he was a floundering teenager. He tried college twice, once at San Fernando Valley State College, but that didn't take, then the University of Southern California; same thing.

"It just didn't click," he admitted. "I guess I was a born salesman, and they didn't teach you sales courses in college."

Mike became a will-o'-the-wisp. At one time he became a fashion consultant for Hart Schaffner and Marx. He was put to work pushing turtleneck sweaters and double-breasted jackets—not simultaneously, of course.

Then he decided to do the outdoors bit and got into speedboat racing. In 1967 he was head of the team that won the Lake Havasu, Arizona, outboard (speedboat) world championship.

In 1970 he married Pamela Putnam, a dental assistant from Atlanta, Georgia. Pamela's father was Duane Putnam, a former Los Angeles Rams football star. But this marriage lasted only one year before it broke up.

Five years later Mike married Colleen Sterns. Cameron Reagan was born three years later, to become the first grandchild of the fortieth president.

"I haven't had a name in the thirty-five years of my life,"

Mike Reagan said during his father's campaign for the presidency. "First I was Ronald Reagan's and Jane Wyman's son. Then I was the governor's son. That's why I want my dad to be president. I've been the governor's son since 1966 and it's time I moved up a station."

Once he had settled down, more or less, Mike began selling boats rather than racing them, but found that boring. When the oil crisis became worldwide and caused huge lines at gasoline stations across the country, Mike decided to get into the oil business through the side door—by marketing gasohol equipment to farmers in California.

Agricultural Energy Resources was established and Mike began selling stock. He also joined forces with a man named Richard F. Carey, to market stock in a company called Sawyer Adecor International, Inc.

He learned quite rapidly that it was less easy as the son of a famous father to do business without repercussions than it was to start up something as a nobody.

By the time his father was elected president and in office, Mike became the subject of journalistic interest reminiscent of the type to which the Nixon brothers were subjected during their brother's administration, and the kind of interest and accompanying press coverage to which Jimmy Roosevelt was subject when his father was president.

Mike Reagan was accused of using his connections with the White House—in other words, the name of Reagan—in furthering his own ends.

There were several separate instances.

One of them involved his own company, Agricultural Energy Resources. An official of a competing company claimed that Mike had sold corporate stock in his gasohol equipment company before it had been lawfully incorporated. And, the allegation continued, he had spent up to $17,500 of the funds invested to support his personal living expenses.

In a separate charge he was accused of steering investors to a man named Richard F. Carey, and persuading them to invest in a company called Sawyer Adecor International, Inc.

The claim was that Mike Reagan and Carey had exploited Reagan's role as the son of Ronald Reagan to persuade potential investors to buy stock in the company. And, it was alleged, he also led other potential investors to believe that Richard F. Carey was the son of Governor Hugh Carey of New York, which he was not.

Mike Reagan was also accused of taking commissions on stock sales when he was not properly registered in California as a securities salesman.

These were serious charges, and they were answered in the only way they could be: by a White House statement.

"The president is confident that the charge will be proven to be baseless. It is a local matter, handled by local courts in California."

Mike Reagan seemed to be off the hook—but not for long, unfortunately. Within weeks another charge was leveled against him. This one was made by the *Oklahoma City Times*, which dug up the story and produced a letter to demonstrate how young Reagan had used his father's name to help a company for which he worked sell hardware to the air force.

The company was Dana Ingalls Profile, Inc., a manufacturer of missile and aircraft components in Burbank, California. Mike was a vice-president of sales for the company. The buyer was Tinker Air Force Base, located near Oklahoma City. Tinker serviced *Air Force One* and other presidential jets, along with many other aircraft. The base usually bought about $2 billion worth of aircraft parts each year by competitive bid.

The letter Mike sent had this paragraph in it:

"I know that with my father's leadership at the White House, this [county's] Armed Services are going to be rebuilt and strengthened," he wrote. "We at Dana Ingalls Profile want to be involved in that process."

Before writing the letter Mike Reagan had phoned Colonel Tom Nash, the air force officer in charge of the purchasing division at Tinker. In the call Mike had said, "We need a stronger national defense. Maybe dad can help." Nash was puzzled by the remark. Who was "dad"? It was not until he got Reagan's letter that he understood who "dad" really was.

Shortly after the receipt of the letter, word got around to the *Oklahoma City Times* and the letter was secured from Tinker under the Freedom of Information Act. Then the story broke.

Guidelines had been established during the administration of Jimmy Carter regarding the use of family influence in dealing with business associates. They were instituted by President Carter to control the myriad affairs of his brother, Billy.

"While it could be argued that members of the president's family have the same right as any other citizens to have the government engage in discretionary dealings with them, this is a right that is best relinquished during the president's incumbency," the guidelines stated.

It was in defense of these guidelines that the newspaper criticized the actions of Mike Reagan in using his father's name to try to influence Tinker to deal with Dana Ingalls Profile.

However, a statement from the White House immediately pointed out that the guidelines developed for the Carter administration were no longer in effect under the Reagan presidency.

"The use of the president's name in his [Mike Reagan's] correspondence was a reference in that letter to a conversation that he had had with the individual [to whom] he was writing," a White House spokesman said.

The president, the spokesman went on to say, did not have "any problems" with the way his son was conducting his business. He said that he hoped his son could "do business as a private citizen without the family name constantly being raised." In fact, he pointed out that his son "should have the opportunity to do business as a private citizen without the problems of his being related to the president of the United States interfering."

Son and father conversed on the telephone when the story broke. Mike claimed that he was being "hounded" by the press. Later, in a television interview, he referred to the *Oklahoma City Times* as *Pravda*, a reference to the Communist party newspaper in the Soviet Union.

He said that the news media was making it impossible for him to find any work at all because of his relationship to the president. "I have got to make a house payment, a car payment, raise a child," he said.

At one point the president gave his son this piece of advice: "Don't write any letters."

The First Lady was more positive—in a negative way—about Mike's actions.

"I think he made a mistake in writing the letter," she told a *New York Daily News* reporter. "I don't think he should have written it. I think he realizes that."

Within the week, Mike Reagan resigned his executive sales job at Dana Ingalls Profile. He made a statement to the effect that he felt he might damage the company's chances of winning government contracts because of his relationship to the president.

"Everyone in the industry is waiting for that B-1 bomber," he said, referring to one of the air force's latest developments. "All the machine shops throughout the country are going to be very busy with that contract. We didn't want my being at Dana to stop the possibility of Dana getting some of the bids and subcontracts for building the B-1."

The *New York Times* took a far more serious view of the matter than did the president in his "Don't write any letters" quip.

"There will always be presidential kin who will try to bully or charm their way to special treatment," it commented, "and plenty of sycophants to oblige them. But a clear statement of principles would induce restraint on some relatives and stiffen backbones of some bureaucrats. Michael Reagan may not be writing any more letters, but his father should put his own rules in writing, and soon."

The *Times* continued: "In fact, the most surprising aspect of the Michael Reagan affair is that it occurred so soon after the protracted Billy Carter mess."

In conclusion, the paper stated: "For their own protection as well as the public's, these officials, be they defense contract agents, diplomatic staff or tax collectors, need the word from the highest authority that favoritism or its appearances won't be tolerated."

Mike Reagan was getting his share of the spotlight he had always felt focused near him. But now its intensity was much stronger than it was when he had told a reporter sometime earlier:

"After a few years, you get used to it. I think you go through a period in your life when you resent it. It hits you the first time you're playing in a football game and someone says, 'Let's get him, he's Reagan's child.'

"People expect you to do better than the next person because your mom and dad are so-and-so. Your first reaction is to get mad at your family. How dare they do this to me? After a time, you try to understand how it evolved. But that's my cross to bear. Now, I enjoy it."

Or, at least, he *tried* to enjoy it.

The prickly situation in which Ronald Prescott Reagan, Mike's brother, found himself during his father's successful bid for the presidency was of an entirely different nature.

Thirteen years younger than his brother Mike, Ron seemed molded in the general stereotype of the square middle-class rich young man when he enrolled at Yale University in 1976. After all, his godfather was actor Robert Taylor. Who better to set the tone of upstanding, front-on, middle-class morality? But then his whole outlook changed.

He became fascinated with the world of dance and immediately plunged into it with enthusiasm and total dedication.

He was 18 years old at the time—quite an ancient for the typical dance professional. Most start studying at the age of 12.

The upshot of his sudden interest caused him to drop out of Yale and move to New York City to work and study. There he made the rounds like any other aspiring actor or member of the entertainment fraternity.

Finally he found himself a place in the Joffrey II "farm team" of the regular Joffrey Ballet Company.

In Russia the public would have applauded. There ballet is an art, a tough game, a respected form of creativity. But Ron was becoming a ballet artist in America, land of muscle-beach jocks and beer-drinking longshoremen. And that raised a few eyebrows. Hairline fractures began showing on the carefully constructed Reagan campaign. Tremors assailed the team trying to elect him. The opposition press sharpened its pencils and went to work. No need to comment; in the United States it is hypothesized that any man who goes into ballet is gay. In spite of the fact that literally thousands of male dancers are heterosexual, the current ethos connects dancing with homosexuality. No logic to it; it's just the American way.

With rumors surfacing about Ron's possible homosexuality and gay relationships, the Reagan campaign team apparently started actively and spiritedly countering that rumor with the facts: the presidential nominee's son was in fact living with an unmarried female lover! And this relationship—obviously the kind of thing any other presidential nominee would suppress and try to keep well covered—seemed to become the rallying cry for the Reagan team!

Ludicrous.

But the candidate was not amused. "Reagan's an incredibly macho man," one of his aides observed. "When he puts on that cowboy hat, he's not kidding. He really thinks he *is* John Wayne. There are probably five million other things he'd rather have his son be."

But Ron would not back down. He had made it on his own.

He liked the life he was living and he was going to pursue it.

And pursue it he did, with his live-in girlfriend, Doria Palmieri, and all.

Then, just before his father was inaugurated—but after he was elected—Ron and Doria were married, and continued to share their live-in apartment as man and wife.

"I don't care about being famous or anything like that," Ron said. "I just want the personal satisfaction of being respected by other dancers. That's what's good about ballet— no one can say you're only there because of who your father is. You can either do it, or you can't."

He could and did. Linda Winer, cultural affairs specialist at the *New York Daily News*, wrote that he was no classical stylist in the traditional mold, but "in the right drama, he has a stage presence."

Clive Barnes, of the *New York Post*, said that he had "enormous dignity" in not buckling under pressure of being the son of Ronald Reagan.

Working with the Joffrey II, Ron wasn't about to get rich overnight. He was making $90 a week, which escalated to $270 on tour. However, with his father elected on a campaign platform of budget reform, he might well be part of the pruning being planned for the funding of the performing arts.

Even so, as well as things went for him professionally, Ron caught some heat during the campaign. He was interviewed by a magazine writer and wound up being quoted as saying that he thought Jimmy Carter had "the morals of a snake."

And so, when it came time to "change the guard" with the Secret Service agents assigned to the president's kin after the inauguration, Ron threw a get-acquainted party for them.

Chip Carter, former Presidential First Son, remembering the remark about his father attributed to Ron in the magazine article, took it upon himself to send a little gift to each one of the Secret Service agents who had been on his old bodyguard detail and were now on Ron's.

Each guard who attended got a pink tutu.

Not everyone was amused. The First Lady later complimented her son Ron for making the adjustment to First Family status extremely well. Although there were plenty of people who would probably like to use all the president's children in some advantageous way, Ron most certainly "might have had the most difficult time" in adjusting—"because of what he's doing."

Shortly after the inauguration, in fact, the President and the First Lady traveled to New York to see their son Ron open in the Joffrey II dance troupe in a star-studded black-tie gala given at the Metropolitan Opera House.

No, neither of the Reagan kids really fitted in with the typical role their father played on the screen before becoming a politician and then a President of the United States. But then, who does, anyway?

2
Big Brother Should Be Watching!

Jimmy Carter's presidency catapulted his brother, Billy, into notoriety. Billy had always been a thorn in Jimmy's side anyway. Involvement with Libyan sheiks, with the IRS in the peanut warehouse scandal, and with his own alcoholism affected not only his brother's administration but international politics as well.

Billy was never simply an influence peddler; he had more imagination than that. As early as the first year of Jimmy Carter's White House occupancy, Billy knew what he was: First Brother and First Clown.

In his role as First Clown, Billy made over a half million dollars in 1977, touring the country on speaking engagements and promoting himself as Second Man in the First Family.

The more Jimmy appeared as the intelligent, worldly-wise, dignified statesman, the more Billy played the foil to him as the loose-talking, beer-drinking, irreverent yokel. Or, in Billy's words, "the token redneck."

Billy was the youngest of the four Carter offspring. Named William Alton Carter III, after his grandfather, he was spoiled outrageously as the baby of the family. He grew up extremely close to his father, James Earl Carter.

He got along gorgeously with his mother, too. In fact, he was able to handle Miss Lillian a lot better than Jimmy could.

She did admit once that she thought Billy drank a little too much beer, but she said that she never tried to make him stop. "I like Billy just like he is," she said. "If he ever tried to change, he'd be the biggest mess that ever was."

When Jimmy ran for the presidency word went out that the reason for the extra effort he put into everything he did was sibling rivalry; that Miss Lillian loved Billy best and Jimmy was simply trying to even things up and make her love him too.

"I don't think that's right," Miss Lillian said. "I think Billy needs my love more. I just *like* Billy. I like what he does, and he looks after me as much as he can."

Billy didn't have it so easy growing up, even with Miss Lillian on his side. He wasn't able to talk right at first. He stammered and mixed up his words. She coached him religiously to try to get him over it.

At one time Billy had to read aloud with a lighted candle in front of his mouth; if he blew out too much air, the flame went out. How many candles he burned down nobody really knows. Eventually he licked his stammer and began talking fluently. In fact, once he got started, he never really seemed able to stop.

During his growing-up years, Billy ran around and wasted his time rather than study. When he was in high school he had defied the authorities by drinking beer on the grounds. For that the principal threw him out. Several years later he returned to finish. He wound up at the bottom of the class.

When Billy was only sixteen, in 1952, he suffered a trauma: His father died. His older brother, Jimmy, was now an officer in the navy. Jimmy felt that Billy wasn't old enough to head the family; so he returned from the navy and took over the operation of the peanut warehouse their father had started. Billy was miffed. He felt that no one in the family trusted him. With Jimmy now firmly in the saddle, Billy decided he had had it. He ran away in 1955 and joined the U.S. Marines. That same year he met Sybil Spires and married her.

The marines didn't change Billy much. In uniform he played the part of a typical two-fisted roughneck. He once tried to take on five or six sailors in a bar over some argument.

"I found out I wasn't as mean and tough as I thought," he recalled.

The service life finally got to him and he left the marines in 1959. On his return to his home in Plains, Georgia, he got into construction work. There were already two children, Kim, born in 1956, and Jana, born in 1959.

After a while he got a job selling paint in a store in Macon, Georgia. His family continued to expand. Buddy, his first boy, was born in 1961. By now Billy realized he had to get himself an education. Everyone else in the family had gone to college, even if briefly. And he hadn't.

He went to Emory University in Atlanta, but college life didn't take. He moved his family back to Plains in 1963, and started helping his older brother around the Carter Warehouse.

Marle, his fourth child, was born in 1964, and Mandy, in 1968. He had one more child, Earle, born in 1977—after the excitement of his brother's move into the White House.

Over the years since his discharge from the marines, Billy Carter had managed to make himself into an image that captivated his friends and nonplussed his enemies. He had a lovely gift of gab. Nothing pleased him more than sitting around in a gas station or store and talking with his friends.

29 | Big Brother Should Be Watching!

To Billy there were two kinds of people—"rednecks" and "good old boys."

"A good old boy," Billy said, "is a guy that rides around in a pickup truck and drinks beer and puts the cans in a little bag. A redneck's a guy that rides around in a truck, drinks beer, and throws the cans out the window."

And he was a redneck, by his own admission.

Meanwhile, Jimmy Carter was becoming a big name in Georgia. In 1962, about the time Billy was trying to make up his mind whether or not he wanted to have a college education, Jimmy had already won an election for the Georgia State Senate. He spent four years in office. He tried for the governorship in 1966 and lost, but then in 1970 he became governor of Georgia.

The glory of it rubbed off on Billy. He got to be a favorite of the newspaper and electronics journalists, who loved to hear him talk about Jimmy and about the Carter life-style.

Billy was delegated to take over the Carter Warehouse and run it. His mother and brother shared most of the ownership of the warehouse—85 percent of it, to be exact. Billy owned only 15 percent. He didn't like that. He thought he deserved at least 33⅓ percent—and maybe even more—for running it. But nothing happened. He was stuck with the 15 percent. But he began running things, and finally worked it up into a $5 million enterprise. He had a good business head.

Almost overnight everything was to change.

In 1976 Governor Jimmy Carter decided that he would try for the White House; he did, and the campaign put Billy back into the news once again. His sense of humor had improved with the years; he knew how to say quotable things.

On one television interview during the campaign he described his brother and his sisters:

"I got one sister who's a Holy Roller preacher [Ruth]. Another wears a helmet and rides a motorcycle [Gloria]. And my brother thinks he's going to be president [Jimmy]. So that makes me the only sane one in the family."

Sane or not, he got the press. "Since [my brother Jimmy] is running for president, he drinks Scotch," Billy told one interviewer, "and I've never trusted a Scotch drinker."

Billy was well aware of the physical image he was portraying in the press: sweat shirt, flapping slacks, sneakers, horn-rimmed glasses. There was no one exactly like him. Sloppy, loose-lipped, laughing, he appeared once in front of an audience and said, "I refuse to reveal the name of my tailor." Openness, frankness, letting it all hang out—his shirt tails as well as his thoughts—that was Billy Carter.

Miss Lillian once summed him up—and herself as well: "I know exactly what he's going to do. I know what he's going to say. I never thought about this before; he must be very much like I am. He tells it just like it is, regardless of the circumstances."

Once Jimmy was in the White House, Billy knew where *he* was going—and that was *out* of the Carter Warehouse. He had to leave, in fact. Jimmy's controlling interest in the warehouse was placed in a blind trust executed by Charles Kirbo, an Atlanta attorney favored by Jimmy.

Billy didn't get along with Kirbo at all. Everything he did he had to check through Kirbo. The two never seemed to agree. "Kirbo," Billy said, "made decisions I was unaware of and questioned every decision I made."

There was no keeping Billy down. Once he was out of the warehouse business he bought himself a gasoline station on the main street of Plains. Tourists came hundreds of miles—thousands, in fact—to buy gas at Billy's filling station, just so they could say they bought gas from the president's brother.

Billy began to get enormous press, drinking beer in the street, laughing with the tourists, and making friends with everybody. In October 1977, with his brother in office less than a year, Billy came up with his first big business deal. He launched a beer—Billy Beer—brewed by the Falls City Brewing Company of Louisville, Kentucky.

Billy Beer Day occurred on October 31, 1977. A rock band from Macon, Georgia, appeared with Larry Hudson and the

31 | Big Brother Should Be Watching!

Stylists, singing a new song, aptly titled "Billy Beer." There were all-day peanut games: peanut tossing, peanut relay races, peanut shelling and eating contests, peanut guessing contests, and a "Peanut Olympics." Even Miss Lillian appeared wearing a yellow Billy Beer T-Shirt.

Billy got plenty of invitations to appear at events all over the country. He hired an agent, Tandy Rice, who booked him on tour like a movie star. In the first year—not including the money from Billy Beer Day—he grossed over half a million dollars!

But Billy's very success was making a pesthole out of his comfortable paradise. He couldn't walk down the street of Plains without having a half dozen people stop him to talk; utter strangers rolled up to him and shook his hand.

And there was more. Officials of the Internal Revenue Service became interested in every business deal he made or tried to make. Soon he was being subjected to all sorts of interrogations.

"I considered myself to be a private individual who had not been elected to office and I resented the attention of different government agencies that I began to hear from almost as soon as Jimmy was sworn in," Billy said.

Billy was put through ten separate investigations, including several by the IRS. His private life was spelled out in the newspapers. And the IRS found that he was about $130,000 in arrears on his income taxes! But that was long after most of the investigations had been made.

Billy's Amoco gasoline station, an eyesore typical of the southern landscape, was becoming a mecca for tourists. The notoriety that Billy was attracting bothered Plains. It bothered Billy, too. Hordes of strangers milled about the place. There were those who walked into Billy's house without even knocking!

He finally decided to move. In Buena Vista, a town twenty miles from Plains, he purchased a $300,000 house.

Then in the fall of 1978 the Federal Bureau of Investigation began looking into the records of the Carter Warehouse, and nice juicy loans of about $4.6 million were discovered, made by the National Bank of Georgia, of which Bert Lance had been president at the time of the loans.

There were rumors that at least half a million dollars of that money had found its way into Jimmy Carter's 1976 campaign. And there was a published story that said Billy Carter had helped falsify the payments of the loans by changing the dates the payments were made.

He was accused of "cooking the books" at the Carter Warehouse. After an investigation by an Atlanta grand jury, Billy went into a personal nosedive. He began drinking heavily and wound up at the Long Beach Naval Medical Center for treatment of alcoholism.

But he bounced back fairly quickly. Never one to let the grass grow under his feet, Billy, in 1978, was globe-trotting in order to secure crude oil from Libya for a company in Jacksonville. And in January 1979 he hosted visiting Libyan representatives.

The oil deal fell through. Billy, however, wound up $220,000 richer. He got one check from the Libyans in December 1979, for $20,000, and another for $200,000 on April 1, 1980.

What did he get the money for? the press suddenly wanted to know. Was he using his position as the president's brother to influence U.S. policy toward Libya, a country with which Washington maintained frigid relations?

There were hints that Billy was trying to get a release on a sizable number of U.S. aircraft that the Libyans had purchased but could not move out of the country because of State Department opposition. Was Billy involved?

Eventually he appeared before a Senate subcommittee, testifying that he had not profited illegally by his trips to Libya; that the money was part of a business loan to him from a bank in Libya.

However, now that he was on the griddle, his public appearances were over. He complained to the Senate that all the negative publicity about the Carter Warehouse had prevented him from making half a million dollars in 1978. He told the senators that he was angry and bitter; his means of livelihood had vanished. Because of his shortfall of funds, he told them, he had gone on the sauce again. That was the reason he needed the money from his Libyan friends—"to help me get back on my financial feet."

Finally, in December 1980, the president was interviewed at the White House on what had become known as the Billygate affair—a play on words recalling the Watergate affair during Nixon's term.

The president said that he had had no advance warning about his brother's dealing with the Libyans. He said that he had first learned of his brother's 1978 trip from his secretary, when Billy was already en route to Libya, and had immediately directed his national security adviser, Zbigniew Brzezinski, to remind the State Department that Billy was not an official representative of the U.S. government.

The president also said he did not know about his brother's second trip to Libya in 1979 until after it had been publicly announced in the press. However, he said he had advised Billy several months before that such a trip would be unwise, because it might be an embarrassment to them both.

The president said that at no time had there been any discussion about the release of any U.S. aircraft to Libya. Nor, he added, did he know that his brother had been engaged in business negotiations with the Libyans, nor that he intended to borrow money from them.

The Billygate affair blew up just before election time. Shortly after Carter lost the election to Ronald Reagan, Billy was told by the IRS that he owed $105,123 in back income taxes for 1978, and would have to pay the bill immediately.

He was ordered to put his Buena Vista house and the fifty-eight acres adjoining it up for auction to raise funds. However, Billy scraped up a "substantial" amount of the bill and paid it off, with a promise that the balance would be forthcoming soon.

Then Billy took off for San Diego, again to dry out.

Both the Libyan connection and the campaign connection faded out of the news. No formal charges were ever made on either allegations of influence peddling. With Jimmy out of the White House, Billy was no longer able to use his brother's influence.

Although far less charismatic than Jimmy's brother, Billy, Richard Nixon's brothers Donald and Edward managed to cause the Watergate president a great deal of trouble during his presidency.

Francis Donald Nixon was the third Nixon boy, and Edward Calvert the fifth. The first, Harold Samuel, died in 1933 of tuberculosis, and Arthur Burdig, the fourth boy, died in 1925 of tubercular meningitis.

Francis Donald, usually called Donald, was always the more friendly, affable, and likable of the five Nixons. His attitude has been described by some as "bumptious," both in inclination and in execution. He seemed never to be too concerned about where his actions would take him.

Edward Calvert, usually called Ed, tended to be more a Nixon type—reserved, quiet, uninclined to pushiness and presumption. Although never as brooding and secretive as his older brother Richard Milhous, he never grabbed the headlines the way either of his other brothers did.

When Richard M. Nixon was serving as vice-president under Dwight D. Eisenhower, from 1952 to 1960, Donald was not above using his brother's name to help enhance his own business efforts.

In 1956, when his brother was running for reelection as vice-president, Donald, then a young stockbroker in Los Angeles, formed a company called Enterprises of F. Donald Nixon. The idea was to solicit funds from Young Republicans to help his brother's campaign.

As if that wasn't embarrassment enough, Donald then founded a chain of restaurants in California, trying to exploit his brother's political clout by marketing fast-food "Nixonburgers" at roadside stands. The franchise operation foun-

35 | Big Brother Should Be Watching!

dered. Then, when Donald was almost a quarter of a million dollars in the hole, he borrowed $205,000 from Howard Hughes—using a tiny $13,000 vacant lot as collateral.

In the end, the Nixonburger chain failed. Unfortunately, the loan and its details returned to serve as a heaven-sent campaign issue for the Kennedy advisers during the 1960 presidential election. Again, when Nixon ran for governor of California in 1962, the story of the loan surfaced to haunt him. It was said to be one of the issues that may have contributed to the Nixon loss.

When Richard Nixon's star rose in 1968 and he was elected president, Donald began using his presidential connections in order to secure other lucrative government contracts—at least so it was reported. One story said that presidential aide John D. Ehrlichman headed off at least two such attempts.

Then Donald suddenly appeared in the Dominican Republic, accompanied by John Meier, one of Howard Hughes's closest aides. Donald and Meier met with President Joaquín Balaguer to discuss the possibility of obtaining a franchise to mine copper.

News of this rendezvous caused a flap in the White House. Almost immediately the president called in his close friend and confidant Charles G. (Bebe) Rebozo for help. Rebozo brought pressure to bear on the Hughes organization and the Hughes people in turn ordered Meier out of the country. He was then forbidden to maintain contact with Donald.

Almost in desperation, the president asked his longtime friend J. Willard Marriott, founder of the Marriott Corporation, a hotel, restaurant, and food-catering firm, to give his brother some job that would, hopefully, be "noncontroversial."

In January 1970 Donald was named public relations vice-president for the Marriott organization. Almost immediately Donald appeared in Athens with a group of Greek colonels and representatives of Olympic Airways. With the magic of the Nixon name, Donald persuaded Olympic to award a contract to Marriott to do all the airline's in-flight catering.

During his years of activity in business circles, Donald had met Robert L. Vesco, a millionaire financier notorious for his involvements in political campaign contributions. In 1971 Donald's son, Donald A. Nixon, went to work for Vesco.

In 1972, when the president was running for reelection, Vesco wanted to contribute $200,000 to his campaign. Apparently he went to Donald who advised him to contact John Mitchell, then head of Nixon's reelection campaign.

However, the transaction immediately aroused interest in the Securities and Exchange Commission. A Vesco aide informed Donald that an SEC investigation was likely to expose the contribution. He wanted Donald to warn the president. Donald testified later that he had not told the president directly, but had been instructed to pass the information on to Mitchell.

Donald's activities covered a number of enterprises. He was said to be involved in dozens of operations, everything from a line of plastics being peddled in Asia by the gigantic Mitsubishi International in Japan to a $4.7 million air force housing development.

"I don't know whether he's got *vice-president* on his business card or *brother*," complained one business competitor. "But Don Nixon sure does get the doors open."

Donald shrugged it all off as political talk. "It's legitimate," he told a magazine writer. "It's all legitimate—every bit of it."

Legitimate or not, the president apparently had some doubts about his brother's efforts. From the first months of his stay in the White House, President Nixon had ordered the Secret Service to put a wiretap on his brother. The tap was placed on his brother's telephone at Newport Beach, California, in the home he used for an office.

When the story of the wiretap broke in the press, the president explained that it was simply part of the "protective function of the Secret Service" that is authorized for the president and the First Family. However, according to the Secret Service, neither Donald nor the president's other brother, Edward, had even been under its specific protection.

The chairman of the Senate's Secret Service Oversight Subcommittee vented his displeasure at the revelation in public. "I think it despicable to wiretap anybody under the guise of security for the president!" said Senator Joseph Montoya of New Mexico.

The statement was made some months before the Watergate tapes were instrumental in Richard M. Nixon's resignation of the presidency.

Congress had passed a ban against nepotism in 1967; the law prohibited a public official, including members of Congress, from appointing or influencing the appointment or promotion of relatives in an agency in which the official serves or over which he has control.

Edward Nixon, the president's youngest brother, had become a navy pilot during World War II, and had trained as a geologist after leaving the service. He moved from job to job, showing evidence of administrative abilities, even though he did not display the flamboyance and aggression of his brother Donald.

Then, in 1969, after his brother Richard was in the White House, Edward was offered an excellent job in Alaska, where he would serve as chairman of the Federal Field Committee for Development Planning. It was Secretary of Commerce Maurice H. Stans who had suggested him for the job. The salary was excellent—$36,000 plus a $9,000 cost of living allowance.

The one mistake Stans made was in not checking the appointment with Ed Nixon's brother, the president. When the president did hear about it, he told the press that he was "very pleased." But . . .

"We have a problem that has arisen at home," Ed told the press. He then went on to explain that he had changed his mind "strictly for personal reasons—a family thing." He said he thought he would be better off living in Seattle, working with the telephone company.

But the truth of the matter was that the appointment had been called off because of a possible conflict with the 1967 ban against nepotism. Again, it was one of the president's advisers, John D. Ehrlichman, who had decided the appointment would raise ugly questions.

Ironically, it was Maurice Stans and John Mitchell who were charged later with attempting to fix a Securities and Exchange Commission investigation of Robert L. Vesco in return for a $250,000 campaign contribution. Both Donald and Ed were called to testify at that trial.

But the court found that the Nixon brothers' activities were not extensive. "My role in the campaign was strictly limited to the political side," Ed Nixon said. "I was instructed to take any finance matter to Stans."

As for Donald, he said: "I never talked to my brother [the president] about anything, and John Mitchell was the man that I was assigned to."

With the resignation of Richard M. Nixon from the presidency, the Nixon brothers faded from the public consciousness. The Vesco connection with the campaign funds never was satisfactorily explained.

By then, nobody really cared anymore.

The Nixon brothers gave little evidence of sibling rivalry in their entanglements with business and politics and with their older brother, as did Billy Carter—and so too Sam Houston Johnson, the younger brother of the thirty-sixth president of the United States.

Sam Houston's relationship to Lyndon B. Johnson was almost a duplication of Billy Carter's relationship to Jimmy. Its cause was somewhat different.

In the case of Billy Carter, he always felt that his older brother got all the breaks; to even things out, Billy sought to establish close ties with his father. He succeeded.

In the case of Sam Houston Johnson, he knew his mother favored Lyndon as her firstborn. In the eyes of some, it was

Rebekah Johnson's failure with Sam Houston that started him on his way to irresponsibility and alcoholism.

Rebekah did lavish all her affection and love on Lyndon, and had little of it left over for Sam Houston. Yet Sam Houston was a bright, likable young boy, although somewhat on the quiet side. He would obey orders without argument and he had the ability of appearing cheerful even on blue days.

After attending Southwest Texas State Teachers College in San Marcos, just like his older brother Lyndon, Sam Houston decided he needed a law degree. He was accepted at Cumberland College in Williamsburg, Kentucky, and graduated there several years later. He then returned home to Johnson City, Texas, but never started his own law practice. Instead, he got a job helping his brother, Lyndon. In fact, most of Sam Houston's efforts in life were in support of his older brother.

Intermittently, for the next twenty years, he was working by his brother's side or near his brother in Washington. He knew Lyndon Johnson intimately. He knew his good side and his bad side. It was during those years that Sam Houston once observed: "Anybody who works for Lyndon Johnson deserves the Purple Heart."

He could have been talking about himself—and perhaps he was. But the cross Sam Houston bore was not the cross of self-pity; it was the cross of alcoholism. He had learned early in life that whiskey could help him assuage his sorrows, at least to a degree. Alcoholism was not the total extent of Sam Houston's inability to cope with life. He seemed also to develop an inability to function in a completely responsible manner.

His escapades began getting into the papers. Because Sam Houston was so closely associated with his brother, who was now a rising young congressman on the Washington scene, Lyndon decided that Sam Houston should be relegated to a less visible position on his staff. Sam Houston was to be the little brother who wasn't there. That was hard, yet in those days Sam Houston almost ceased to exist outside his brother's aura. The press seemed cooperative in keeping him in the shadows.

A man with no identity sometimes goes out of his way to call attention to himself. Was that the reason for Sam Houston's refuge in alcohol? Perhaps it was his way of awarding himself the Purple Heart deserved by everyone who worked for Lyndon.

Lyndon himself tried to help. The Senate leader rarely got smashed, but one afternoon on the golf course the game had been broken up by rain, and Lyndon wound up with a fellow senator in an adjoining bar. He came home soused.

Lady Bird tried to steer him to bed, but Johnson shook her off. He wanted to see his brother. Sam Houston had gone to bed, Lady Bird told him.

"Just leave me alone, Bird," Johnson told her and staggered up the stairs, crashed into his brother's room and turned on the light.

Sam Houston stirred and squinted at the formidable Lyndon towering over him with a loose grin and disheveled clothing.

"I want you to take a damned good look at me, Sam Houston," Lyndon shouted. "Open your eyes and look at me. I'm drunk, and I want you to see how you look to me, Sam Houston, when you come home drunk."

"Okay, Lyndon," Sam Houston sighed. "I've seen you."

Even if the lesson was a graphic one, it didn't change Sam Houston much. He was, however, an excellent wheeler-dealer; a man who could get things done behind the scenes to make his brother look good. And Lyndon knew just how to use him.

Typical of one of their brother-act ploys was the deal they got for one of Johnson's staff writers. The staffer got an excellent offer from a rich Texas industrialist who wanted an image maker and speech writer. The Texan approached Johnson, telling him he wanted the staffer.

Johnson was annoyed; nobody ever quit on him. The staffer was reluctant to leave; he talked to Sam Houston.

"He's offered me twenty thousand a year—that's three times what your brother's paying me."

"Check with Lyndon," Sam Houston suggested.

"What if he won't let me go?" agonized the staffer.

"You've got to take the chance."

The staffer called Lyndon. "How much is he offering you?" Johnson asked the staffer.

"Twenty thousand a year."

"That's not enough," said Johnson. "Tell that old bastard he's got to give you twenty-five thousand dollars plus another five thousand for expenses—otherwise I won't let you go."

The staffer repeated Johnson's exact words to the Texan. The Texan thought a moment: "Why, sure!" he boomed. "I think that's a right fair figure. When can you start?"

Sam Houston told Johnson what had happened. Johnson laughed, then said, "Hell, I should have said thirty plus five!"

In 1958, during Lyndon's later years in the Senate, Sam Houston suffered a bad fall in his kitchen, fracturing his hip in the process. His recuperation didn't proceed normally. A bone in his leg was seriously infected. Sam Houston had to undergo major surgery that left him with one leg four inches shorter than the other.

It was an affliction that led to his own retirement from Washington. He returned to Texas. But when Lyndon landed in the White House after the assassination of President Kennedy in Dallas, Sam Houston flew back to the capital as his adviser.

Once again Johnson repeated his earlier stratagem of keeping his brother in the background. Yet no matter how hard he tried, it never seemed to work. Sam Houston always managed to pop up, like a grinning jack-in-the-box, to throw sand in the presidential machinery.

In 1964 Sam Houston was responsible for a quotation attributed to the president in a national magazine that almost derailed his brother's campaign for reelection.

There was talk of nominating Senator Sam Pastore of Rhode Island as Lyndon's running mate. Sam Houston gave this juicy riposte to the suggestion, claiming he had heard Lyndon say it: "How can an Italian from a stinky state like Rhode Island possibly help me?"

The flap that ensued brought Lyndon out waving his arms and crying "misquote!" Of course, he told the press, his brother had only *thought* he heard him say that. What Sam Houston did hear, he didn't know.

Later that same year Sam Houston was recovering in a Myrtle Beach hospital from a lung infection. He hired a private nurse to look after him, and paid her with two checks, one for $180 and another for $198, written on the Austin National Bank of Austin, Texas. Both checks bounced.

When Sam Houston failed to pay the nurse, she brought legal action against him to collect her $378. The police appeared, and a worried Sam Houston hired an attorney from Conway, South Carolina. Immediately the money was paid to the nurse. The warrant for Sam Houston's arrest was withdrawn. The attorney told the press that the whole affair was a simple "mistake on the part of the bank."

"I have been told," he said, "that it was a bookkeeping error. The whole thing was entirely unnecessary."

The Austin National Bank made no comment on the matter.

Soon though, he was back in Washington. During Johnson's 1964–68 term in office, the president installed Sam Houston on the third floor of the executive mansion. And from there the kid brother gave his advice on various matters to the president. And he was a man who always had plenty of advice to give. Sometimes Lyndon didn't particularly like it. But Sam Houston didn't believe in being anything but frank with the president.

"You don't come across on TV, Lyndon," Sam said. "You

ward to alcoholism, to a suspicion of madness, and to eventual dissolution.

Teedie, for all his weaknesses of physique, became a sun that sparkled brightly, a fountain of energy, ebullience, gusto, and an advocate of simple fun in living the good life.

Elliott went down and down until he could sink no further.

Teedie went up and up until he had attained the seat of power in a world that loved and respected him.

Why was there this difference between them?

In spite of his handsomeness, Elliott was born with a susceptibility to head pains and seizures. So tormented was he by them that at times he screamed aloud.

In 1875, while at private school, Elliott had what he called "a bad rush of blood" to his head; he fainted and was removed from the school. Did he have some form of epilepsy? Apparently not: The fits of dizziness were too infrequent to fit such a diagnosis. Were they physical manifestations of a psychological inability to cope?

After a year of illness Elliott was sent by his family out to Texas to live the outdoor life with a friend of the family. There he learned to ride and shoot. He fell in love with hunting, in the form of wild-turkey shoots, and sent letters home about his exploits.

When Elliott's father died in 1878, his brother Teedie took over the leadership of the family. Teedie and Elliott were close; Elliott visited his older brother frequently at Harvard. But he never really thought he could follow in his brother's academic footsteps.

By now Elliott had found a way to assuage his bouts of physical pain, which had not diminished during the years. He took to drinking heavily and associating with a wild set of friends.

Inspired by Elliott's letters from Texas, Teedie wanted to see the West. Elliott took him out to meet his old friends. By the time the two brothers returned to New York, Elliott had decided that he was going to India to hunt the tiger and the elephant, and to the Himalayas to find the ibex and markhor.

He wanted to escape. Teedie was competition. Teedie would be running the family. Elliott had no talent for being second.

In the Himalayas he was struck down by what the locals called the "fever," but which was obviously a return of his earlier seizures. The attack was such a fierce one that he had to abandon the expedition and return home. No ibex or markhor were to be hung on his trophy walls.

What was this mysterious malady that kept afflicting him, this "rush of blood to the head" that made him cry out in pain? Most of Elliott's contemporaries, including his doctors, thought of it as a weakness for alcohol—a weakness that was not rare in those days.

But in Elliott's case, his "malady" was much more powerful than alcoholism. Indeed, it was beginning to erode his personality. Medical evidence indicates that he may have suffered from a brain tumor which first became active during his childhood.

Elliott strove to overcome the constant, nagging pain with physical activity. But simple exercise did not do the trick. Only alcohol seemed to dull the constant pain. He caroused in the fashion of the time, and escaped the pain. A few years after his return from India, he was established as the town's most visible high-rolling sportsman, polo player, and drinking companion.

Then for several years a new interest overrode even his own pain. He met and courted Anna Rebecca Hall. She was a tall, slender beauty, "a great belle," as he described her. Even during his courtship, the seizures recurred.

"My old Indian trouble," he called it with a faint smile.

Anna was worried about the sudden depressions and melancholy moods. But Elliott fobbed them off. They were married in 1883 and very soon became the most attractive and watchable members of all the New York "swells"—as the tabloids dubbed the very social and very rich.

But Elliott's malady persisted, and so did his refuge in alcohol. Anna had sensed it during their courtship; now she knew her husband had a serious problem. Cold and scornful of frailty of any kind, she simply assumed that her husband was weak-willed and a slave to a filthy habit.

In spite of Elliott's growing dependence on alcohol and on Anna's growing revulsion to him, they had three children: Anna Eleanor, born in 1884, who was called Eleanor and who later married her cousin Franklin Delano Roosevelt, of the Hyde Park Roosevelts, to become a First Lady in her own right in 1933; Elliott, born in 1889; and Grace Hall, a boy who was always called Hall, born in 1891.

During those years, Elliott continued his frenzied sportsmanship with his many friends. He was rarely around the house. His main occupation was in keeping up with the Meadowbrook crowd, a group of hard-drinking, hard-riding young hellions.

One day he was involved in a hunt that began at the Mineola fairgrounds. Forty riders started out. Thirty-nine dropped out, with only Elliott following the huntsman. At the end of the run he was thrown from his horse and fractured his collarbone.

Later on, while he and friends were rehearsing for an amateur circus, Elliott was practicing a double somersault and broke his ankle. The physician misdiagnosed the break as a sprain. Elliott lived in pain for weeks. He could eat nothing and at night he would sob for hours in bed.

The physician eventually had to rebreak the leg and set it again. During his extremely painful recuperation, Elliott became more dependent than ever on alcohol, using it to dull the constant physical torment that assailed his body.

Anna, who had just borne Elliott, Jr. in 1889, was disdainful and icy with disapproval at her husband's weakness. Their relationship was at a new low. A year later, to recreate harmony, the couple decided to go to Europe, starting a long tour in Berlin. From Berlin they went to Munich, and on to Vienna and Italy.

Anna was pregnant again, with the child due in June. By June they were in Paris. There Elliott had a sudden relapse. He vanished for days. When he returned he seemed depressed, penitent, guilt-ridden, and full of promises to reform. Then he went off again, to pub-crawl and return shattered in body and spirit.

After the birth of Hall in June 1891, Elliott seemed to go to pieces completely. In desperation, Anna and Aunt Bamie, who had rushed to Paris to be with Anna, had him committed to an asylum for medical treatment. Elliott complained that he had been "kidnapped."

It was a no-win situation. Anna wanted a divorce; Elliott promised to stay under the care of doctors for six months at an institution outside Paris. Anna and the rest of the family sailed for home.

Once home, Anna applied to the courts to have her husband adjudged insane; she requested that his property be placed in trust for his wife and children. Sadly, Teedie and Bamie told the court that Elliott's physical and mental condition had deteriorated considerably. They mentioned that their brother had three times threatened to kill himself.

Elliott found out what was happening. He wrote a letter to the courts protesting his family's action. Eventually Teedie was forced to make a trip to Paris to persuade his brother to take a treatment for alcoholism. When he arrived, Teedie found his brother in much worse straits than he had thought. Elliott was living with a mistress in Paris.

Teedie had to argue and protest for hours to get Elliott even to agree to come home. The woman with whom he was living did not like Teedie or his interference. She later wrote that Elliott looked bruised and beaten down by his brother. In the long run, Teedie won out. Elliott returned to the states and took a five-week "Keeley cure" for alcoholism at Dwight, Illinois.

Once released, he was shipped off to Abingdon, Virginia, where his sister Corinne and her husband, Douglas Robinson, lived. The Robinsons were delegated to try to straighten him out.

In 1892 his wife, Anna, died. Before her death she had persuaded her sisters and aunts to take care of her children if anything happened to her. She particularly wanted them kept out of the hands of her estranged husband.

On her deathbed she made her own mother official guardian of her children, begging the Halls to deny Elliott any rights of a father. The children were shipped off to New York. Then, in 1893, young Elliott, Jr., died of scarlet fever.

Eventually Elliott was allowed to see his two remaining children, but only briefly. He would meet his daughter Eleanor and take her out with him in a horse-drawn carriage for drives around the city. One day he took her and three fox terriers he had with him to the Knickerbocker Club where he stayed. He went in the club, telling Eleanor he would be back in a moment. He had promised to take her and the dogs for a ride. Hours later she was still sitting outside, waiting for him. He never did appear.

Actually, he was removed from the club room in a state of total inebriation and put to bed. The doorman took care of Eleanor. She was hurt by her father's absence, not understanding his condition and assuming he had deserted her.

Soon Elliott began leading a double life. He would tell Corinne that he was returning to Virginia, but ten days later he would still be in New York. He lived in a hotel, but no one could find him there. He even disappeared from the places he usually ate and drank. His mail was delivered to the Knickerbocker Club, but he was not there either.

Eventually he was tracked down to an apartment at 313 West 102 Street. He was living with a woman whom no one in the family knew. From this tawdry sanctuary, Elliott wrote letters to Eleanor and Hall, promising them drives around the city.

In Washington, where he was serving as assistant secretary

of the navy, Teedie wrote a letter to his sister Bamie: "Elliott is up and about again; and I hear is drinking heavily; if so he must break down soon. It has been as hideous a tragedy all through as one often sees."

On August 14, 1894, Elliott was injured in a fall, was knocked unconscious, and did not recover. He died that same day, moaning for his sister Corinne.

In the *New York World*, a story told of his death, revealing that he had been living on West 102 Street for some time, known only as "Mr. Elliott." Most of the family, the story went on, did not know that he was living in New York.

"Few of them had seen him for a year," the article said. "At the clubs no one knew his address. Even the landlord from whom he rented his house knew him only as Mr. Elliott."

For ten months he and his valet had lived there, when he sought absolute seclusion.

"Many people will be pained by this news," the story went on. "There was a time when there were not many more popular young persons in society than Mr. and Mrs. Elliott Roosevelt."

Elliott was buried at Greenwood Cemetery.

Brain tumor? Epilepsy? Alcoholism? No one will ever really know what caused the disintegration and eventual dissolution of Elliott Roosevelt.

But he was connected, as few have been, by two direct ties to the First Family of America:

He was the brother of the twenty-sixth president.

He was the father of the thirty-second First Lady.

Presidents William McKinley, Ulysses S. Grant, and Andrew Johnson had bad press because of certain activities of their brothers—although none was as deeply neurotic or failed as abysmally as Elliott Roosevelt.

Abner McKinley was the younger brother of the twenty-fifth president, born six years after him. He was almost a William McKinley look-alike—and that wasn't at all bad. It was generally conceded that McKinley's dignified and matinee-idol image was what got him twice elected; it may even, in a perverse, psychotic way, have been what got him killed by an assassin, if we accept the modern psychological interpretation of hubris.

All his life Abner knew exactly what was going on around him. A calculating and shrewd person, he loved to take risks; he loved to play with money in a daring way. He knew that one could easily step over the bounds of legality if the fact was not discovered. He learned to attend to the precepts of religion and morality his mother had taught him so that he could know what facets were the easiest to discard.

His domestic life was impeccable. But when it came to business, Abner's attitude was that of a slick and sharp speculator: if it made money, it was good business.

A promoter, Abner lived in New York in high style at the Windsor Hotel on Fifth Avenue. He had a summer place in Somerset, Pennsylvania. He, his wife, and children were early versions of the Beautiful People.

Along the road to riches, Abner had picked up a reputation for always keeping an eye to the main chance. Rumors surfaced. One hinted that he had once made a pile of money selling worthless railroad bonds at high rates. Another said that he had turned a tidy profit on telegraph stock that was totally worthless.

Charles G. Dawes, one of the men responsible for getting William McKinley into the White House, knew Abner inside out. When Abner once approached Dawes to try to persuade him to put money into a new scientific process whereby artificial rubber could be made more cheaply than the real thing, Dawes knew there was something fishy about the proposition.

After Abner explained in elaborate detail the so-called secret process, of which one requirement was a period of total darkness for the chemicals to "turn into the artificial rubber," Dawes smiled faintly. "That was when they put the rubber in," he told Abner.

During his brother's presidency, Abner appeared frequently at the capital, trying to work deals with members of the White House staff. He was noticed.

The *New York Evening Post* charged that Abner was trying to dispense patronage and peddle influence through his blood ties to the president. But the McKinleys were smart enough not to let the thing escalate into a full-blown scandal. Who was bought off and who was paid to keep his mouth—or pen—quiet is not known.

Orvil and Simpson Grant, Ulysses S. Grant's brothers, were always considered bigger successes by their father than Ulysses was—at least, until the Civil War started.

Simpson died before Grant became president, thus saving his administration from one brother with his hand out. But Orvil was still alive and flourishing. It seemed that every time Grant turned around at the White House, there was Orvil looking for a favor.

Grant had little compunction about giving his friends and relatives appointments to various governmental agencies. And he gave plenty of favors to Orvil. By count the records show that he awarded him at least four specific appointments that were cushy or semicushy!

There was plenty in the newspapers about it, too; Grant was attacked constantly for his nepotism and for his "morally indefensible" acts, one of which involved Grant's secretary of war, W. W. Belknap.

A word of explanation is in order here. Most of the army posts of the era were established on or near Indian reservations in order to keep the Indians from hitting the warpath. The government, through the War Department, controlled the various military posts—like our modern PXs (post exchanges)—where goods, including food and clothing, were sold to the army officers, to the public, and to the Indians on the reservations nearby. The man in charge of the army post was in a beautiful position to make himself a rich man very quickly. No one else could come in and compete with him. The profits were all his to control.

Because of the inherent value of being in charge of such a money-making post, an appointment became a choice plum for any man. In fact, later scandals erupted when it was learned that men in the government bureaucracy actually *sold* these posts to anyone who could pay the going rate, pocketing the money for themselves rather than putting it into the public till.

Orvil Grant didn't even have to pay for the post he got. Belknap *gave* him one of the most lucrative, probably after some chivvying by the man in the White House. Later on, it was said, Orvil sold it to someone else, pocketing the take himself!

Howls were loud and sustained when this bit of nepotism was discovered. By then Grant was becoming involved in so many other scandals that Orvil wasn't made a martyr to the press. He simply faded away—with his pockets loaded.

William Johnson was very close to his brother Andrew, who became the country's seventeenth president, after the assassination of Abraham Lincoln. As a boy in Raleigh, North Carolina, Bill was always running somewhere, usually away from home, or away from the tailor to whom he was apprenticed. He even got Andy, also an apprentice, into trouble several times.

When he was sixteen, Andrew and another companion were caught tossing gravel against a pretty young girl's window. Andrew knew he was in bad trouble. With his brother Bill he ran off, taking two other apprentices with him. The four wound up in Carthage, fifty miles southwest of Raleigh. There they boldly opened a tailoring business of their own.

However, the Raleigh tailor to whom they were apprenticed issued a "wanted" warrant for their arrest, offering a ten-dollar reward for their return. They came back to Raleigh, and Andrew settled down. But Bill took off and vanished somewhere out west.

Later, when Andy got to the White House, Bill, like the bad penny he was, turned up in the capital. The president decided to buy him off the quickest way he could: He pinned a U.S. marshal's star on his chest, and sent him down to the wilds of Texas.

Nobody ever remembered what happened to Marshal Bill Johnson.

But they remembered what happened to his brother, Andy. He was the first president ever to be put up for impeachment in the U.S. Senate.

There was never any real scandal about Thomas Jefferson's younger brother Randolph, largely because Randolph never left the South to go up to Washington with Tom.

Actually, he couldn't make the trip. He was always slow-witted and simple-minded. He was not the only one in the family to be so afflicted. His sister, Elizabeth, was mentally retarded; and his mother had some zany streaks in her make-up.

Randloph Jefferson was a slow learner, a backward pupil. He was said to be "a might simple man," who "used to come out among the black people, play the fiddle, and dance half the night," according to one source.

The slaves on the Jefferson plantation at Monticello said that he did not have too much more sense than some of the slaves—that was their quiet way of pointing out he wasn't up to scratch, from a white man's standpoint.

Jefferson continued to help Randolph all through his life. Randolph never gave his older brother Thomas much trouble. He married and had a sizable family. Jefferson helped them make ends meet at Snowden Plantation, one of his holdings located a few miles from Monticello. Randolph's inability to function without constant supervision were early hints there might be strains of mental retardation in the family line.

Later on we'll see how these strains affected his mother, Jane Randolph Jefferson, and his sister, Elizabeth Jefferson.

55 | More Sad Bad Glad Mad Brothers

* * *

George Washington's family was a mixed bag. In all there were ten children, including George—three girls and seven boys. Lawrence was the steady one, George's favorite brother. He died in 1752, when George was twenty years old.

John (Jack) Augustine Washington then became George's favorite brother. Aside from George, he was the only other real winner in the clan. He became a prosperous planter who married well and and raised a successful family.

It was Charles and Samuel who gave Washington the most sleepless nights. The youngest of the line, Charles grew up quickly, succeeding, in his teens, in becoming one of the heaviest drinkers in the county. Throughout his life he continued to spend much of his time involved in unproductive pursuits of all kinds.

Samuel, however, was a greater problem than Charles ever was. Samuel loved to run through things—especially women and money. During his lifetime he was married five times, a prodigious effort in early America. He produced a variety of children through his various wives.

A friend once compared him rather favorably to Henry VIII. Samuel Washington was the total profligate, spending money on everything that struck his fancy, and running his own family deeply in debt. Because he was continually facing financial ruin, he was always trying to borrow money from his older brother George. Washington usually refused. He didn't have much money to spare, even though he was well fixed.

Once when he was being hounded by Samuel for various loans and other kinds of assistance to help him out of difficulties, George fired off a letter to his favorite brother Jack, in which he let out all stops in blasting the profligate brother.

"In God's name!" he exploded. "How did my brother Samuel contrive to get himself so enormously in debt? Was it by making purchases? By misfortunes? Or sheer indolence and inattention to business? From whatever cause it proceeded the matter is now the same, and curiosity only prompts me to the enquiry, as it does to know what will be saved and how it is disposed of."

Quite likely, after that outburst, George may have broken his standing rule and again advanced money to his improvident brother, to bail him out in the name of family charity.

In his will George Washington fixed it so that his executor would be able to pay off several of Samuel's outstanding debts and clear some property that Samuel had mortgaged to the hilt.

Samuel died still owing money—and a great deal of thanks to his more provident brother.

4

Am I My Sister's Keeper?

Generally speaking, sisters of presidents do not become the problems to their brothers that brothers do. But in the case of Jimmy Carter, he happened to have two sisters, each of whom became characters in their own right.

Gloria is the second oldest Carter offspring, right behind Jimmy. She was always known as the "pretty one" in the family. Called "Go Go" in her early years, she was considered the sexy one, the one the boys liked to follow around.

She was more than that. She was a very good athlete, and she loved to play all the games the boys played—only she played better. She was the first on the block to ride a motorbike and she was always excellent in any competition demanding coordination and competition.

Her personality was easy to take, too. Her mother once said that she admired Gloria because she was her own person and did what she wanted to do.

"I don't think there's anything about you I'd like to change," Miss Lillian told her daughter once. "You'd pay no attention to me anyway, and that suits me fine."

After finishing high school in Plains, Gloria Carter went to Georgia Southwestern State, where she studied journalism. In those years World War II had brought dramatic changes to the South. There were soldiers everywhere, in training for combat.

At an air base near home, Gloria met an air force enlisted man named Everett Hardy, called "Soapy" by his friends. His career prior to the army had been unimpressive: He had spent most of his time behind a counter as a soda jerk.

In 1945 Gloria and Soapy eloped and moved from place to place as Soapy tried to get a job. He failed at finding work in the same manner he failed at making his marriage work, and four years later Gloria divorced him and returned to Plains with their son William, who was called "Tody."

In Plains Gloria met another man, Walter Spann. Spann was a better provider than Hardy. After they married, Gloria moved onto his successful farm, trying to bring up Tody and trying to make her second marriage work better. The marriage prospered; the boy did not.

From the beginning, it was obvious that Tody was "different"—incorrigible, slow to learn, and rebellious. Gloria and Walter enrolled him in a special school that provided therapeutic aids and other counseling he needed. Even though Spann was well-off, Gloria got a job as a secretary in order to help pay for Tody's expensive treatment.

The boy made his mother's life a nightmare. When he was a teenager he would drift off for days on end. Then, when he came home, it would be in the small hours of the morning. He was kicked out of school in the eighth grade, and once again was relegated to special classes.

Although Tody was in the hands of psychiatrists, they seemed unable to do much for him. Spann adopted him formally, but nothing seemed to give the boy any feeling of self-confidence. He seemed bent on self-destruction. He hated his stepfather; and tried to make a fool of his mother.

Jimmy Carter, Tody's uncle, once gave him a job driving a company truck at the Carter Warehouse. Tody appropriated the truck for a joy ride into the next state and abandoned it. Then he took off and didn't return for days.

By then Tody had begun to live on the road. He bummed his way around the country, picking up with all kinds of vagrants. Soon he was into drugs, homosexuality—which seemed to be the root of his problems—and petty theft.

Frequently he would telephone home to announce that he was in jail again. All this torment began to tell on Gloria Spann. But when her brother Jimmy decided to run for the presidency, it all came to a rather sordid head. Gloria became the target of blackmailers.

One in particular called her on the telephone, threatening to reveal the truth about her son to the press if she didn't pay him hush money. Gloria refused to pay. The blackmailer did release the story to the media, which printed and broadcast it. However, in the 1960s the public had become inured to drug busts, homosexual demonstrations, and freedom of expression, so there were no repercussions that really hurt Jimmy Carter's campaign bid. He was elected in spite of these "truths." After all, as Gloria said, the voters were voting for Jimmy, not for Tody.

The boy eventually graduated from petty theft to armed robbery. He was arrested, charged, convicted, and jailed. By that time he had become an avowed homosexual.

But the trouble and the embarrassment was not over for Gloria even yet. After her brother's inauguration, Plains became a mecca for tourists. Gloria's brother Billy bought and ran his famous Amoco gasoline station in the center of town, flogged Billy Beer, and sold souvenirs.

The Spanns bought an acre of ground in the middle of Plains and began marketing it—square inch by square inch! It was a clever gimmick. Each square inch sold to any tourist who wanted to buy it was registered and recorded in Sumter County. The story got into the papers and onto television. The gimmick seemed to be a big hit with the public.

Unfortunately, to Jimmy Carter's political enemies, it looked like a perfect target. They zeroed in on it, calling it a scam to bilk people out of their money by selling them worthless property. What could an American citizen do with a square inch of Georgia ground?

The White House reverberated with shock waves of reaction. Jimmy's advisers got together and decided to shut down the Spann operation. Jimmy was authorized to tell his sister Gloria that she would get him into real trouble if she and her husband didn't stop the real estate ploy.

They stopped it. It was the only tourist operation in Plains connected with the presidency that Jimmy objected to. It was a true embarrassment all around. First Tody—now this, called the "Big Inch Connection" by the amused media.

Ruth Carter was the third Carter child and the second sister of the clan. She was almost as good at sports and athletics as her sister, Gloria—but not quite. She was her father's favorite child. Ruth could always get Earl Carter to do anything she wanted him to. She had a father fixation on him that was noticed by many observers of the family.

Her mother, who spoke her mind about everyone anyway, spoke about Ruth many times too:

"I admire her persistence in the work that she's doing," she said, referring to Ruth's evangelical and faith-healing activities. "She never gives up. In spite of hardships and the criticism she gets, she just keeps on going."

Miss Lillian thought about that character trait. "That's about all I admire about Ruth," she went on. "She's not a very good mother, but her family just adores her, so I reckon she's all right."

Ruth Carter went away from home to Georgia State College for Women in 1946. There she met Robert Stapleton, who was studying to be a veterinarian. They were married in 1949, before Ruth finished college.

The marriage was in rocky shoals almost from the beginning. Stapleton could see the handwriting on the wall: He would be part of a triangle with definite Oedipal overtones if he and Ruth lived in or near Plains. He would be competing eternally with Ruth's father. Ruth's relationship with her mother was likewise a complicated one: The two of them were always at each other's throats, largely because of Ruth's preference for her father.

Ruth didn't see it that way at all. She wanted to live with her family. Stapleton wavered at first, but finally decided that he could not permit Ruth to be so near her other love. When Stapleton finally delivered his ultimatum, Ruth caved in, and the Stapletons moved to Fayetteville, North Carolina, 450 miles away from Plains, where Stapleton became a successful veterinarian. They had four children—two boys and two girls: Lynn Stapleton Nimock married and settled down in Fayetteville. Patti Stapleton Alligood also married and stayed in Fayetteville. Scotty Stapleton was a medical student at the University of North Carolina, and later became a doctor. Michael attended Appalachian State University in Boone.

Ruth began seeing psychiatrists and trying to straighten herself out. She had been suffering bouts of depression. It was during one of them that she experienced what she later called a "rebirth."

Contrary to the public's belief that rebirth is a flash of insight, Ruth found it to be quite the opposite. To Ruth, being "born again" meant "to come into a spiritual awakening, to accept the consciousness of Christ.

"Very seldom," she said, "do I see a dramatic experience. Ninety-nine percent of the time it's a very gradual change within you and you never, never know exactly when the awakening happens."

Nor did being born again alter Ruth's life immediately. It

was a gradual change. One simplistic way of describing her "conversion" would be to state that she found that if she could lay her whole burden before Jesus Christ, the weight would be alleviated, her depression lifted, and her psychic wounds healed.

"It's up to each person how much he or she grows," she said. "This is a process that goes on for the whole rest of your life. And it affects everyone's life differently."

Her own "rebirth" occurred shortly after the birth of her fourth child, Michael, when she was in a state she called almost "total desperation." She wrote in her best-selling book *The Gift of Inner Healing*: "I was gripped with the illusion that I was a hopeless failure—as a wife, as a mother, as a person."

Her renewed faith in Jesus Christ lifted her depression. "I turned almost immediately to a commitment of service." And the service was trying to help others work their way out of depressions and suicidal morasses. To help others, she wrote books and counseled people in person. She founded the Inner Healing Center, in Fayetteville, North Carolina. The name of her evangelic organization became Behold, Inc.

Ruth had grown up a Baptist, but in her rebirth she reasoned that she would have to work outside the established religious denomination: She felt Jesus Christ looked on people of *all* religions and did not exclude those of any sect or group.

Naturally, this did not sit well with ministers of the various established religions. She was immediately tagged as a "false prophet," and other apellations. One Alabama minister called her a "witch disguised as an angel of light."

None of her activities kept her brother Jimmy from being elected president. However, after he moved into the White House, several of Ruth's activities *did* get him into trouble.

The first action was Ruth's friendship with Larry Flynt, the publisher of *Hustler*, a rather outspoken magazine deemed pornographic by some. She had converted him and later celebrated Thanksgiving with him and his family. That started a flap in the White House.

Ruth never apologized for the Flynt episode. But another incident did cause a great deal of trouble.

Sam Bamieh, a businessman and president of Industrial Development Group, Inc., of Palo Alto, California, became a member of Ruth's board on Behold, Inc. Bamieh became friendly with Ruth and helped her on various projects.

IDG was a financial and marketing consulting firm, involved in the management of exports. A $110 million business, it was about eight years old at the time Bamieh became a director of Ruth's group. One of the things IDG was involved in was buying properties and materials in the United States for "Arab interests."

In 1980 Ruth got in touch with the White House and the State Department to help arrange a trip to Egypt, Jordan, Oman, and Saudi Arabia. The members of the trip would be Ruth Stapleton; Cliff Curtis, a friend of Ruth's and a minister; Bamieh; his wife, Nida; and John Calhoun, an officer of IDG. The purpose of the trip was a business-oriented swing through the Middle East.

The trip took place in January 1980. By the time the party got to Jordan, the U.S. State Department representative there, Nicholas A. Veliotes, warned Ruth that she was being "used" by Bamieh. Obviously he meant that Bamieh was exploiting her closeness to the president in his contacts with the local businessmen.

In Oman, Marshall Wiley, also a U.S. diplomat, likewise warned her that her association with Bamieh would get her in trouble later on.

When they returned to the United States, all hell broke loose. Enemies of the White House claimed that Bamieh had paid for the trip in order to get business deals he couldn't have managed without the presence of Ruth Carter Stapleton and her blood ties to president Jimmy Carter.

But Bamieh didn't pay for the trip, Ruth protested. He

paid only $3,000 of the total amount. She and Cliff Curtis had put up $8,000.

"I was told by the State Department when I called," Ruth said, "that it would be very wise if I accepted not one single penny from the U.S. government and that I accepted not one single penny from any foreign country."

She also said that she had been warned about these "complications" before she had ever started.

"She told me," Jody Powell later told the press, "that she realized she had been used."

Bedeviled by the press, Ruth finally blew up at a reporter who telephoned. "They can't hurt me!" she cried. "I am clean!"

The affair soon cooled down and blew away almost without a trace. But both Carter sisters were singed by their closeness to Jimmy Carter and that very hot heat in the White House "kitchen" that Harry Truman used to talk about.

Rosemary Kennedy's affliction was never really a problem to her brother at the time of his presidency. Her affliction was of quite a different kind from those of the Carter sisters.

She was one of whom it could easily have been said: She always marched to the tune of a different drummer.

Rosemary had been a slow learner, even as a child, but it was not discovered until her late teens that she was mentally retarded. Up to that time she had been sheltered in the family as just another child—Joseph P. Kennedy's third, born just after John F. Kennedy.

In the Kennedy clan competition was always understood and practiced. But Rosemary simply did not compete. Nor did she push herself forward. She was quiet and restrained. And after a number of years had gone by, it became obvious that she was retarded mentally.

The Kennedys sent her to St. Coletta's School in Jefferson, Wisconsin, in 1941. However, even in those rather enlightened days, the Kennedys did not want it known that she was "different."

The word that went out to the press through the Kennedy public relations mill was that Rosemary had answered "a divine call to a life of religious devotion."

It was not until years later that the truth was finally revealed. Interestingly enough, it was during the presidency of John F. Kennedy that the facts about Rosemary surfaced. Rose Kennedy, her mother, was the one selected to spread the word.

"We had a daughter born about a year and a half after our second son, who later became president," she would say wherever she was speaking, and then she would launch into efforts to help the mentally retarded.

However, the public knew only the partial truth. As a girl, Rosemary had been subdued and passive, but when she neared her twenties, she took a turn for the worse. She began having violent tantrums, smashing objects, and striking people around her.

She had been taken to various doctors to find out what was wrong with her. Her rages were diagnosed as part of a "neurological disease," in other words, as part of some undisclosed "disease of the nerves."

It was obvious that she could not continue in the highly competitive atmosphere of the Kennedy home. There was one step that could be taken, the doctors told the Kennedys. It was surgical, and it was a radical step, and it was irreversible.

At the age of 21, Rosemary Kennedy was prepared for a prefrontal lobotomy operation. At that time drastic surgery, like a prefrontal lobotomy, was sometimes recommended for certain neurotic symptoms. The theory was that by cutting nerve fibers in the brain, some forms of mental illness could be alleviated.

"The operation eliminated the violence and the convulsive seizures," Rose Kennedy wrote in her memoirs, without specifying the type of operation used, "but it also had the effect of leaving Rosemary permanently incapacitated."

That told some of the story, but not all. Rosemary was left with only minimal use of her faculties. Prefrontal lobotomy is not used today except in the most urgent cases demanding radical mind alteration. Psychoactive drugs for hyperactivity are recommended instead. Of course, such tranquilizers were not available for prescription in 1941.

"It's so very sad," said Sister Paulus, Rosemary's companion at St. Coletta's, where she was placed after the operation. "The lobotomy wasn't necessary because with medication Rosemary would have been just fine. But she's very sweet and is taken good care of where she is."

Because of Rosemary the Kennedy family has always been at the forefront in raising money and funding institutions to help the mentally retarded. For example, Eunice Kennedy Shriver today directs the Joseph P. Kennedy Foundation, devoted to the field of mental health.

In effect, the thing that made Rosemary "different" from her brothers and sisters eventually helped bring about public recognition of the mentally handicapped and helped initiate ways to prepare the retarded for life in the real world.

Many sisters of presidents of the United States suffered from various grades of neuroticism. But in the old days these tendencies were dismissed by males with a typical "that's a woman for you" air. Some of these sisters were more neurotic than others.

The dividing line between neuroticism and real aberrant behavior is an extremely fine one. Revelations and admissions of the flaky behavior of ladies in the nineteenth century lay hidden in the attics, back rooms, and closets of American homes. But occasionally some have managed to surface.

Chester A. Arthur was the country's twenty-first president, serving from 1881 to 1885, upon the death of President James Garfield.

When Arthur was about thirty, just before the outbreak of

the Civil War, the country was torn by dissension and whole families were rent by opposing views of the coming conflict. Arthur's family was no exception. His sister, Malvina, was a perfect example. In the years immediately preceding the outbreak of the Civil War, she, a Vermonter, went into the South to take up her profession of teaching.

Arthur's brother, William, kept correspondence with Malvina more fully than did the president-to-be. He wrote once to Chet Arthur to inform him of Malvina's plans. She was, he wrote, "off for down South to locate herself among the niggars."

She was an outspoken, determined woman. In South Carolina, she met and married Henry Haynesworth. During the years of the Civil War, she kept up her correspondence with William Arthur. Once the war had started, Malvina moved north to take refuge with relatives in New York City. But her husband opted to stay in the South where he joined the Confederate army.

In the summer of 1864 Grant was moving toward and threatening Richmond, Virginia. And Malvina's husband, Henry, was right in the path of the Union juggernaut—in Petersburg.

"If Grant has got Petersburg *mined*," she wrote, "and the papers [so] report, I hope you will contrive to let Henry know. I don't want him blown up."

Later on she followed up that notation with another, reminding her brother of his duty: "I don't care how soon you take Petersburg, but *don't hurt Henry*."

Henry managed to escape unscathed, and was joined by Malvina in the South after the war. Henry had some trouble getting relocated after peace was declared; the government favored hiring Northerners rather than Confederates, but he finally managed to get work.

Malvina and Henry visited their brother in the White House when he was president, many years after the troubled times of the Civil War. By that time Malvina's neuroticism was more or less under control.

* * *

Fanny Isabella Hayes was Rutherford Birchard Hayes's older sister. Through a series of catastrophes Hayes's father, oldest sister, and brother had all died before he was fully grown. His mother was a strong-minded pioneer woman, and his sister Fanny Isabella was loving and devoted to him.

Perhaps she was *too* loving and *too* devoted.

She was an intellectual, a lover of romantic novels, a dreamer. Her brother, Rutherford, who became the nineteenth U.S. president, was an intellectual himself. They shared a love of literature and the cultural arts.

While Hayes was away at Kenyon College in Ohio, Fanny Isabella was married in Columbus. Her husband was William August Platt, an enterprising and successful young businessman.

There was trouble almost from the beginning of the marriage. Will Platt was hardly a dreamer like his wife. A hard-nosed merchant, truly excited about commerce and finances, eager to make piles and piles of money, he had no interest in the fripperies of culture.

During her first married years Fanny Isabella began to experience short bouts of depression and gloom. Soon these became of longer duration. Was she yearning for someone close at hand who could share those cultural interests that had been such a positive influence in her younger years with her brother, Rutherford?

There was no question but that Fanny Isabella could relate to her brother much more easily than she could relate to her husband. Obviously there was an invisible triangle in her relationship with her husband that marriage had failed to resolve.

Fanny Isabella's mother, Sophia Hayes, was another factor in Fanny's mental and psychological morass. For one thing, she did not particularly like Will Platt. She thought him an unfeeling and irreligious man, too devoted to Mammon and far too mercenary to be decent.

Sophia was strong-willed in her religious tenets. She believed that anyone who did not share her awe for religion was doomed. And she blamed her son-in-law's lack of religious fervor for the trouble that was brewing between him and her daughter.

In 1841 Fanny Isabella bore a baby girl, Sarah Sophia. Just after childbirth Fanny Isabella suffered almost total amnesia. The doctor attending her did not know whether its cause was physical or "temperamental."

Her amnesiac condition was followed by an intense melancholia. Then her mind blacked out, and none of her family knew what to do. Quite soon, however, she recovered.

"She is clothed in her right mind," her mother wrote. "The prayers of her Friends have been heard."

Once she recovered, she took care of her little daughter. However, in June 1841 the baby died. This time the mother did not suffer loss of memory and orientation. She seemed to acquire an almost stoic attitude to hide her inner grief.

She wrote her brother:

"I knew you must feel our loss as you said you did, for I thought you loved our bright, beautiful child. Time is all that can heal such a wound, yet I feel calm and cheerful."

She was disconsolate for days, but then decided she must interest herself in something else. Writing and reading poetry seemed to help her, she told him.

In 1842 she had another girl, and named her Laura. The birth was an apparently easy one, and all things seemed normal at first. However, some days after the childbirth, Fanny Isabella became, in the words of her husband, "mentally deranged."

She was suddenly afflicted with violent convulsions. The rage and aggression she displayed made it necessary for Platt to tie her to her bed. He described the scene graphically to her brother, Rutherford, who was off at college.

Later on, Platt was forced to have Fanny Isabella committed to what he called a "lunatic asylum." She stayed there for only a short time; her mental condition soon improved and she became herself again. Then she returned home.

It seemed that her mental condition had a lot to do with her deteriorating relationship with her husband. Sophia Hayes, her mother, did not help at all. She kept up a constant barrage of letters to her son about Fanny's husband and Fanny's ill health.

Her animosity against her son-in-law caused her to revert once again to her almost fanatic religious fervor. "To think that our lovely and amiable Fanny should be the companion of lunatics—alas, and one herself—is heartrending," she wrote her son. "She had been too much our Idol and the Lord has seen fit to deprive us of her. Let us bow in humble submission to His will and pray that this sore affliction may be removed from us, and that our darling may be restored to us."

Of course, by the time the letter was written, Fanny Isabella was back home. The child was in good health. The young mother was never better. That fall her husband took her on a trip to the East. She returned, fattened up and amiable.

Her brother visited her on the trip East. He joked about her health to his mother. "It appears to be the object now with fashionable ladies to bring their forms as near as possible to that of a soap tub. In the accomplishment of this, Fanny succeeds admirably, for between the flesh and the padding, she has rendered herself considerably broader *one* way than another."

For a number of years Fanny Isabella enjoyed good health. Then, fourteen years later in 1856, she became pregnant once again, and gave birth to twin girls. The double birth was a tragedy—and a permanent physical blow to Fanny Isabella. The little girls died immediately. And the delivery, which was a terribly difficult one, left her critically ill. After serious infection, other complications followed.

Once again she began to slide back into the same melancholy condition she had experienced in 1842. Her mind began straying. She no longer remembered who she was. She blacked out. Her memory was gone.

At this point her brother was practicing law. He visited her constantly. When she drifted back to awareness, she spoke to him as if she were doomed to die.

Although she rallied and almost recovered, she did not survive one final attack. The end came in July 1856. She was only thirty-six years old.

"Oh, what a blow it is!" Hayes wrote. "During all my life she has been the dear one. . . . My heart bleeds and the tears flow as I write."

Thomas Jefferson's family was a large one with brothers and sisters of varying personalities and characters.

The first of his sisters to be married was Mary, the second oldest, born two years before Jefferson. In January 1760, when she was nineteen, and Thomas was seventeen, Mary married John Bolling.

Mary had never been Jefferson's favorite sister. Nor was Bolling a favorite brother-in-law. In fact, Jefferson could not *stand* Bolling, and took no pains to hide the fact.

The Bollings were constantly at each other from the time they were married. At one time they separated, vowing never to see one another again. But soon they were back together again, scrapping and threatening each other in loud and angry tones.

The problem was fundamentally Bolling's. He was developing into a full-fledged alcoholic. He was "in a state of constant intemperance almost . . . happy only with a glass in his hand," as Jefferson's daughter Maria wrote about him later.

Mary herself annoyed Jefferson, who mentioned her "constant string of little checks and obstacles." And apparently her disintegrating relationship with Bolling caused her to become intemperate in her own way. She constantly criticized and questioned him, especially in company, obviously to shame him.

"I wish my sister could bear his misconduct with more patience," Jefferson wrote. "It might lessen his attachment to the bottle, and at any rate would make her own time more tolerable."

It was not to be, however.

But sadder still was Jefferson's sister Elizabeth, who seemed never to grow up properly. At twenty-one, she still had the mental capacity of a small girl. And as a retarded child, she was an exasperating problem for the family. Even those who loved her had to put up with uncontrollable temper tantrums, disappearances, and other types of aberrant misbehavior. She lived only to the age of thirty. Most of her adult life she was a burden on her sisters and brothers, who had to spoon-feed her and keep her clean.

On February 21, 1774, there was an unusual occurrence in Virginia—an earthquake so intense, according to the records, that it frightened everyone enough to scare them outdoors.

Elizabeth, obviously more frightened than the rest, went absolutely out of her head. While the others were simply scared and running about to see what damage had been done, Elizabeth ran too, out of sight. When a modicum of order had been restored and the members of the family were assembling together at the house, they found that Elizabeth was missing.

Immediately they spread out through the woods searching for her. She was not to be found. Apparently totally disoriented, she had wandered far out of sight and hearing. The wilderness was never a place to be lost, no more then than now, and the Virginia countryside was mostly deserted woodland where there were no homes and farms.

Three days later, on February 24, they discovered her body. What had happened to her and how she had died was never known in detail.

5

Rascals, Rapscallions, and Other Relations

One requirement for anyone who intended to marry into the family of Joseph P. Kennedy was a total commitment to the Kennedy way of life. A Kennedy in-law must be a sports addict, a political ally, and a person of such involvement to the Kennedy persona that his or her individuality had to take a back seat.

Surprisingly enough, most were, but there were exceptions. Most notable was Jacqueline Bouvier, who retained a great deal of her own image even though she became a total Kennedy in other respects. After the death of her husband, however, she rather obviously deserted the clan when she married Aristotle Onassis.

There was another exception. He was not a sportsman, not a politician, not a man who believed in submerging his identity. Peter Sydney Ernest Lawford wasn't even an American, nor was he what counted most with the Kennedy—a Catholic!

Yet in 1954 he married Patricia Kennedy, the sixth of nine children of Joseph P. Kennedy, the patriarch of the clan, or dynasty, as it has been called.

Lawford was an Englishman; and an actor—a profession loathed by the patriarch, who had served some years in Hollywood wheeling and dealing and had little truck with people who spent their lives pretending to be other than they were.

Old Joe did everything he could to break up the match between Patricia and Lawford. He failed, and Lawford became the offbeat brother-in-law to the man who would eventually be the thirty-fifth U.S. president—John F. Kennedy.

Meanwhile, Lawford had made a name for himself in Hollywood. He was a member of the famous Rat Pack, the group that sported such hell raisers as Frank Sinatra, Dean Martin, and Sammy Davis, Jr. In the Rat Pack, Lawford's cognomen was "Charlie the Seal," for no known reason.

When eventually John F. Kennedy did become president, Charlie the Seal became a dead weight, and Jack Kennedy decided he had to give Lawford the brush.

On a presidential flight to Palm Beach, Lawford was hanging around waiting to be invited to the Kennedy house. "Peter, disappear," said the president. Lawford failed to vanish. "All right, where are you staying?" Kennedy asked, implying he would have him chauffeured there.

"Where you stay," Lawford told him.

Kennedy shook his head. "You're not staying with me. Let me know and I'll call you."

Lawford grinned. "I won't hold my breath."

"Don't," replied the president.

And Lawford went his own way.

"Being related to the president of the United States is a very great honor," Lawford said. "But it is not and never will be a career."

Eleven years after their marriage, Lawford and Patricia were divorced—making it the first divorce in the Kennedy family. But by that time, JFK was dead, and Lawford could drift back into the Hollywood fold without making any conspicuous waves.

A brother-in-law of an entirely different sort plagued William McKinley, just before the turn of the twentieth century.

McKinley's wife, Ida, came from a well-to-do banking and business family headed by James Asbury Saxton of Canton, Ohio. The Saxtons had a son, George, who, even in middle age, was known in the Ohio scandal sheets as a very active Lothario. His most notorious affair involved a married woman, Mrs. Anna George.

Saxton had long been self-cast in the role of romantic lover, and in the carefree years of the "Gay Nineties," Saxton did his dashing about on one of the most picturesque methods of locomotion of the time—a bicycle. In his bicycle cap and snappy clothes, he rode about wooing his married lover. Eventually he drove away her husband, Sample C. George. When he left her, George took their two children with him.

Anna set herself up in a dressmaking establishment, and finally brought proceedings against her husband for a divorce. Saxton put up the money for the court case. The divorce was granted, and Anna then sat around in her dressmaking shop waiting for Saxton to come and claim her for his wife.

He never did. Apparently he had tired of her during the weary court proceedings and had found more fertile fields to conquer.

Outraged, and realizing that perhaps she had been made a fool of, Anna accused Saxton of breaking his promise to marry her. A series of rather sordid lawsuits followed, all of which titillated the Ohio public for some months.

One oddball wrinkle in the contests was a court suit

brought by Sample C. George, the cuckolded husband, who sued Saxton for alienation of affections in an attempt to force him to marry Anna.

At this time, Saxton's brother-in-law, William McKinley, was serving his first term as governor of Ohio.

Shortly after the end of the affair between Anna and Saxton, Anna was apprehended by the police trying to break into one of Saxton's offices. She was looking for some of her private belongings, which, she said, he had refused to give back to her. Saxton appealed to the police for "protection" against his aggrieved former mistress.

By the time Saxton's brother-in-law was elected president, the Saxton-George affair was pretty cold stuff and the newspapers were turning to other morsels.

Meanwhile Saxton had found "other fields" to conquer. One was named Mrs. Eva Althouse. Eva was a widow—as attractive as Anna—and Saxton continued to see her during McKinley's first years in the White House.

When Anna George learned about Eva Althouse and George Saxton, she told friends that if Saxton continued his affair with Eva Althouse, she would kill him. No one paid any attention to her threats, assuming that she was hurt by Saxton's attentions to the other woman and was simply working off her jealousy.

On the night of October 7, 1898—in the autumn of McKinley's second year in the White House—Saxton put on his rakish riding cap, light-colored overcoat, and jumped onto his fleet bicycle. Then he pedaled across town to the quiet residential district where the Althouse home was situated.

He parked his bike and crossed the sidewalk to the front walk. As he started up the steps that led up the neatly terraced lawn, there were sudden gunshots. They came from a bush on the property. A tall, slim woman dressed in black was hiding there. As the sound of the shots echoed in the street, the woman in black ran out of the shrubbery and vanished in the night.

George Saxton fell to the ground, wounded by a gunshot in the belly. He was dying.

It did not take the police long to make an arrest. They found Anna George within hours. She was immediately charged with murder and scheduled to be tried.

The president and First Lady rushed to Canton for the funeral. McKinley went to Saxton's grave and bowed his head with the proper solemnity. Later on he met with the county prosecutors to discuss the trial. Ida McKinley, Saxton's sister, remained in seclusion.

The trial of Anna George took place the following April and was the sensation of the year. A huge wave of sympathy had built up for the murderess, who had been ruined and then deserted by the philandering Saxton. Nobody really thought much of the aging libertine who had driven her to her act of revenge.

Anna George took a room in the Williams Hotel, and in her free time, while not in court, embroidered sofa cushions and put them up for sale. They became collectors' items almost immediately. Passersby would wait for her to appear on her way to court, just to get a glimpse of her.

The political implications of the trial became the big news angle of the day. McKinley, because of his relationship to the victim, became a kind of unsympathetic avenging angel. The Democrats hoped that Anna George *would* be convicted. Then they could play up the villainy of the Republican McKinley in her prosecution.

Ironically, the prosecutor, Atlee Pomerene, was a very close friend of McKinley's—but a Democrat. If he won the case, *he* lost sympathy. And if he lost the case, he looked a damned fool—and the Republicans got the advantage.

Ugly intimations surfaced. McKinley was informed by a close friend in Canton that "unsavory evidence" *might* be necessary in the conduct of the trial. These items of evidence obviously had to do with George Saxton's activities, and would redound negatively on the administration.

McKinley's friend, James J. Grant, acting as attorney for Anna George, resigned the job and joined the counsel for the prosecution. None of the "nasty things" hinted at ever got mentioned during the trial's proceedings.

The trial packed the courtroom. People gazed in awe at the accused, admiring her beauty, her modesty, and her superb aplomb. The public loved to hear the Saxton name smeared by the defense. The newspapers took to leaving out parts of the testimony deliberately, terming it "too salty" for publication. That only made the readers exercise their salacious imaginations the more.

Pomerene and the attorney for the defense waged a theatrical battle. Although it was obvious that Anna's guilt was well established by the prosecution, the jury, taking twenty-four hours to make a decision, found her not guilty.

When the verdict was announced to the public, there was a loud and hysterical outburst of cheering from the spectators. The crowd waiting outside the courthouse broke into howls of ecstasy.

Anna George left the courtroom with her every move watched by the public and the press. However, within hours she had vanished from sight in Canton, and was never again seen in public.

No book contracts, no long series of articles in the tabloids, no publicity at all came to Anna George from her act of retaliation.

Pomerene, who was ambitious and had lost the most sensational case of his career, was not surprised at the verdict of the jury—although he knew he had crafted an almost unbeatable, tight case. Even though he had failed to bring about the prosecution of the woman who had killed McKinley's brother-in-law, he and the president remained on the best of terms.

Saxton had been a problem, but he had been a vital and interesting person. His sisters loved him. It was discovered on his death that in 1890 he had made out an annuity of $3,000 for Ida McKinley, if she ever needed it. Then when Ida became First Lady, Saxton had altered this provision in favor of his sister Pina's children.

The First Lady never reacted in public to the verdict—or to the murder itself. It was as if the incident had never occurred. What was so terrible to the First Lady was the fact that the family name had been besmirched by the press. Her reaction to this indignity was only an aloof, prideful silence.

Despite the bad publicity of the murder trial so close to the First Family, McKinley easily won reelection. It became a dramatic irony that murder put an end to McKinley's second term, when he too was the victim of an assassin's bullet, in 1901.

Ulysses S. Grant was surrounded by relatives who gave him sleepless nights. One who contributed a true scandal to the Grant administration was Abel Rathbone Corbin, who was married to his sister Virginia.

Corbin had been editor of the *Missouri Republican*, and had served as a St. Louis alderman. However, he was a man with an eye to the future. In the words of one observer, he was a "slippery, uneasy man of sixty-seven, with his eye on the fleshpots of high finance."

During Grant's first administration, Corbin was involved in a scheme hatched by two stockmarket manipulators in a convoluted plot to corner the gold market. Corbin's associates were the notorious Jay Gould and James Fisk, Jr., two New York operators who had succeeded in wresting control of the Erie Railroad from its rightful owners.

They now proposed to grab up all the gold bullion in the United States, force up its price by calling in contracts to buy, and then selling it off when the price was at its highest. It was a brilliant scheme—and workable at the time when greenbacks were used as money and the paper money pegged at a going rate in relation to the cost of the gold that backed it.

The U.S. Treasury held about $100 million in gold to back

up the paper. Gold was still used by business, but usually in paying off transactions made with other countries. For example, an importer who must pay a bill in Europe would send actual gold coin abroad; the greenback was not well-enough established to be used commonly overseas.

The gold would return to the United States when a European would send it back to buy American goods. The gold was not in actual circulation, but was kept in reserve to back the paper. However, because of trade balances, the price of the greenback fluctuated.

Gould's plan was to make out contracts to buy an amount of gold *in excess* of what the Treasury held. Then, by purchasing blocks of gold, he would drive up its price. Soon he would attract other investors to get in on a "good thing." Everyone would be trying to buy gold, but he would have it all. The price would skyrocket.

Then, when it reached its dizzying height, he and Fisk would unload and make a grand killing.

At the time Gould and Fisk intended to put their scheme into practice, it cost about $135 in greenbacks to purchase $100 in gold. If they could drive up the price to $145 per $100, the profit would be enormous.

There was one loose link in the scam. That involved the federal government, which released for public sale several million dollars in gold each month. The idea was to keep some gold specie in circulation.

When the price of gold began to rise, the Treasury could easily release millions of dollars' worth, and would close off the buying spree. How to get the government to close off the sale of gold on the open market? Perhaps, Gould and Fisk thought, they could arrange it through the president, or the secretary of the Treasury.

The two manipulators found their line to the White House in Abel Corbin, the president's brother-in-law. At a meeting in Corbin's New York residence, Gould set up a meeting with the president. Corbin was in on the scheme. As a payoff, he was to have one million dollars in gold at bottom rates to sell at top rates, and keep the profit.

On one of his trips to New York, the president stopped off at Corbin's house. There Corbin brought in Jay Gould to meet him. At the rendezvous, they set up a later friendly trip on the Fall River Steamboat Line, which Fisk owned.

It was there that Gould and Fisk together tried to con the president into withholding federal gold from the open market until the scam paid off.

It was Jay Gould who worked his wiles on the president. He was worried, he told Grant, about the farmers. The farmers' prosperity depended on the value of the dollar—that is, the greenback. Currently, the gold dollar ran at about $135 to $100 in greenbacks.

But everytime the Treasury released gold to the public, the price fluctuated—going down before it climbed once again. What if the Treasury refused to sell gold for a few months? Wouldn't the dollar—the greenback—rise in price? Maybe to $140?

Of course it would. Then, when gold came in from Europe to pay for the wheat the farmers were selling, wouldn't they make *more* money with the greenbacks at $140 than at $135? Of course they would.

The U.S. should be *getting* gold from Europe, not *sending* gold. Keeping gold was the way to make a prosperous country out of the United States!

Grant demurred. He mentioned the fact that he thought there was just a bit of inflation in the greenback as it was. But he would think about it.

On another occasion Gould and Fisk took the president, the First Lady, and their daughter to the opera in New York. Corbin was there, too. The sight of the president with Gould and Fisk was a calculated public relations ploy. It meant the two financiers were in solid with Washington.

Gould was no fool and Fisk was a shrewd man. Neither of them was utterly convinced that Grant was "in" with their ploy. They were aware that he could pull the rug from under them at the last minute by ordering the Treasury to sell gold.

They almost decided not to try the scheme, but Corbin

persuaded them to go on. He was thinking of the money he would make on the deal. He said he had the president "sewed up."

Grant was in no way sewed up, but in view of Gould's persuasive arguments, he had sent a memo to his secretary of the Treasury, George S. Boutwell, to go easy on selling the gold so as not to force the price of the greenback down.

With some qualms Gould and Fisk began to obtain contracts on all the available supply of gold. The price of gold was at $132 per $100 when they started buying up the gold contracts on the first of September. By the middle of September the two men held contracts for at least twice the available supply of gold. And, as expected, the price began to rise. The purchase of so many contracts caused speculators to sniff out a possible killing; they rose immediately to the bait.

Gold was soon at $140/$100. By now all sorts of smalltimers were getting in on the market. Gould was still not satisfied. He knew the Treasury Department had delayed putting up its gold for sale, but how long would the delay last?

Gold was past $140 and going higher. Gould was now involved to the tune of $50 million. If the Treasury suddenly released gold, he would have to sell at a loss. He decided to pull out. Corbin wanted him to stay in. To assure Gould that Grant was "sewed up," Corbin wrote a letter to the president arguing against release of the gold.

The manipulators had timed things well. Grant was on a two-week vacation in a tiny village in Pennsylvania. The place had no telegraph, so a personal messenger delivered the letter by hand. Horace Porter, Grant's personal secretary, received the letter. The messenger had been instructed to wire back a reply from the president. When Porter took the letter from the messenger, he told him it was "all right," meaning that the letter had been received and would get to the president.

The messenger rushed to the nearest telegraph office in a nearby town and telegraphed Gould that the answer was "all right."

Gould took that to mean that the deal was set, as promised by Corbin. He proceeded to push the price up still higher by buying up more gold.

Meanwhile, Grant had read the letter. The First Lady was drafting a letter to her sister-in-law Virginia at the time. Grant told her to add a postscript to the letter, stating that the president was "much distressed" by her husband's speculations.

"The General says," Julia Grant wrote, "if you have any influence with your husband, tell him to have nothing whatever to do with [Jay Gould and James Fisk, Jr.]. If he does, he will be ruined, for come what may, [the president] will do his duty to the country and the trusts in his keeping."

That is, he would release the gold.

When Corbin got the letter, he showed it to Gould. Instantly Gould knew that Grant was onto the scam; that he had, in fact, never really been "in" with them. He immediately instructed his brokers to sell all the gold he had, without informing Fisk.

Fisk was completely conned, and continued buying up gold, boasting that he would see the price up to $200/$100. Buying and selling was so mixed up that at one time Fisk's brokers were buying at $155 and on the other side of the Gold Room selling at $140.

By noon, September 24, 1869, gold had reached the staggering price of $163.50/$100. Fisk was still taking contracts by the million. On that same day, word came from Boutwell at the Treasury that the government was releasing $4 million in gold to the public.

Within thirty minutes the price of gold had plummeted to $135/$100. Speculators by the thousands were ruined. The sidewalks of the Wall Street area were filled by men who were roaming the byways to find Gould and Fisk with a view to lynching them.

Gould's decision to get out had made him several millions of dollars. Fisk was stripped temporarily. But when Fisk learned how Gould had left him holding the sack, he slapped him on the back and complimented him on his savvy. Fisk always admired a man sharp enough to swindle him.

September 24, 1869, became known as Black Friday. The House of Representatives investigated the debacle a year later, but the Republican majority treated the whole thing very gingerly. The Democrats hinted that Grant was in it up to his neck, but they were unable to injure his still reputable image.

Later on, the full details of the story finally came out. Grant eventually began to lose his reputation for integrity. The fact that a man who was a close member of his family had tried to influence him left a bad taste in the mouth of the public.

Corbin thus became the first relative of a president involved in influence peddling in the White House.

There was one famous in-law who almost brought down the Lincoln First Family even before the House of Booth did.

Her name was Emilie Todd. She was Mary Todd Lincoln's half sister, born eighteen years after Mary. Her mother, Elizabeth Humphreys Todd, was Mary's stepmother; so much friction had developed between Mary and Elizabeth that Mary left the house to move west to Springfield, where she met Abraham Lincoln.

In her White House years Mary Todd Lincoln was a woman of great inner conflicts. She was at heart a Southerner; almost her entire family supported the South. And it was a large one.

She had two brothers, three half brothers, three sisters, and five half sisters.

Her youngest brother, Dr. George R. C. Todd, and her three half brothers, Samuel, David, and Alexander, had joined the Confederate army at the time Mary's husband was president and commander in chief of the Union army. Her sisters Elizabeth, Frances, and Ann supported the South. Her half sisters Emilie, Martha, and Elodie were the wives of Confederate officers, and another half sister was a Southerner in sentiment.

Only her oldest brother, Levi Todd, and her half sister, Margaret Todd Kellogg, sympathized with the Union.

But it was Emilie Todd who was closest to Mary during the grimmest and most rugged years of the conflict. Not only were Mary and Emilie close, but so were Lincoln and Emilie's husband, Ben Hardin Helm, who was a West Point officer and whose father had been governor of Kentucky.

When the war broke out, Lincoln invited his brother-in-law to the White House for a talk. When Helm finally left, Lincoln handed him an envelope containing a major's commission in the Union army.

"Here is something for you," he told Helm. "Think it over for yourself and let me know what you will do." It was obvious what he meant. Southern states were seceding. The war was only days away.

The First Lady kissed her sister's husband and said, "Goodbye. We hope to see you both very soon in Washington."

But Helm chose the South.

Other members of the First Lady's family caused some official embarrassment, at least the way the press played it up. Mary's brother, Dr. George Todd, had become a jailer at the federal prison at Richmond, where the Union soldiers captured at Bull Run were kept.

"He was tall, fat and savage against the Yankees," one newspaper trumpeted, "and so brutal that he would kick the dead bodies of Union soldiers, calling them damned abolitionists."

Charges were brought against him by his own people. Jefferson Davis, president of the Confederacy, had him posted to another site.

Reporters then dug up the fact that the First Lady had eleven second cousins in the Carolina Light Dragoons of the Confederate army. Mary knew nothing about them, had not even heard of any of them. But the newspapers gave a lot of play to the story.

The first one of Mary's family to die in battle was Captain

Alexander Todd, her half brother. He was killed at Baton Rouge.

"Since he chose to be our deadly enemy, I see no special reason why I should bitterly mourn his death," the First Lady said as stoically as she could. How she really felt about the matter was not ever expressed.

Then, on September 4, 1863, Ben Hardin Helm, Emilie's husband, was killed at Chickamauga while leading John Breckinridge's division into battle in a heavy attack against the forces of Major General William S. Rosecrans.

Because Emilie was so close to both the First Lady and the president, Lincoln sent a letter to Emilie's mother to move Emilie and her children from Alabama, where they lived, to Lexington. From there she was conveyed to Washington.

Their reunion was a bittersweet one. But after a few days in the White House, the tensions generated by the war surfaced. Emilie tried to settle into the White House routine without hearing the obvious whispers of the servants about the "rebel" being harbored by the First Lady. Mostly Emilie kept in the background with her children and held her tongue. But occasionally her true feelings erupted.

Major General Daniel Sickles, a Union officer who had lost a leg at Gettysburg, called at the White House with Senator Ira Harris of New York to inquire about the fate of Major General Breckinridge, whom they both knew. Because Emilie had been in the South recently, and because her late husband had served under Breckinridge, she was invited in to see them.

Sickles asked her about Breckinridge, but she would tell him nothing. Nor did she try to hide her animosity toward Sickles.

Senator Harris tried to smooth over the stormy waters, but he did it in such a way that it made things only worse.

"We have whipped the rebels at Chattanooga," he said, "and I hear, madam, that the scoundrels ran like scared rabbits."

Emilie burst out angrily: "It was the example you set them at Bull Run and Manassas."

The First Lady moved in quickly, trying to make peace. But that too was a wrong move. Senator Harris's only son was in the Union army. He knew that Robert Lincoln, the president's son, was not. There had been a great deal of whispers about the First Family's lack of patriotism—rumors focused on Robert Lincoln.

"Why isn't Robert in the army?" Harris asked sharply.

The First Lady, who had moved heaven and earth to keep him out, explained quickly that he was not a shirker, but that he was in college. "If fault there be," she said, "it is mine. I have insisted that he should stay in college a little longer."

Senator Harris responded with a reminder that his one son was fighting—apparently forgetting for the moment that he was not making a political speech. He added that if he had twenty sons, *all* would be fighting rebels.

Emilie interrupted angrily: "And if *I* had twenty sons, they would all be opposing you."

She stormed out of the room, dissolved in tears. Sickles hobbled upstairs to visit with the president, who was recovering from a mild case of smallpox.

"You should not have that rebel in your house!" he exclaimed wrathfully after repeating what had happened downstairs.

Lincoln calmed down Sickles as best he could, but he knew that he would have to send Emilie back home. After a few more weeks of visiting, Emilie left in December.

The president said his farewells with all the proper dignity and emotion. Putting his arm around her shoulders, he said, "I tried to have Ben come with me."

Emilie acknowledged his kindness, but said she would never change her allegiance to the South any more than her husband did.

The Lincolns saw Emilie again the following year, not at the White House but at Soldiers Home. Emilie was desperate for help. She told Mary that her brother Levi—he was Emilie's half brother—had died. There was simply not enough food and sustenance for the people in the South. The irony was inescapable. Levi actually favored the Union forces.

Levi was, she said, "another sad victim to the prowess of more favored relatives." She meant the Lincolns, of course. She herself, she said, was suffering from want. Her cotton crop was picked but had no buyers. The South was destitute. Could the president bring out the crop and sell it in the North for her?

Lincoln had to refuse. Some of the most infamous scandals of the time had to do with cotton deals between Southerners and Northerners. His enemies would have driven him out of the White House if he had acceded to Emilie's wishes.

Emilie knew what she was asking. "If you think I give way to excess of feeling," she told him, "I beg you will make some excuse for a woman almost crazed with misfortune."

But the president could not help her.

It was a sad and touching impasse.

Lincoln's enemies would not let up. The presence of Emilie Helm in the White House had given them fuel for their fulminations. The Lincolns had harbored a traitor in the White House. After Emilie's departure, the tune changed slightly—and became more sinister.

Now the evil-wishers whispered that the First Lady herself was a traitor. *She* was in the White House, poisoning the president's mind against his own people.

Lincoln was beside himself with anger. In an independent move, he appeared before a hearing of a Senate committee on treason and made a statement.

"I, Abraham Lincoln, president of the United States, appear of my own volition before this committee of the Senate to say that, I, of my own knowledge, know that it is untrue that any of my family held treasonable communication with the enemy." Then he stalked out.

His visit brought an end to the committee's work but not to the whispers that continued to echo about Mary Todd and her relatives. Her enemies were at it even after the war ended and the president fell to an assassin's bullet.

Civil War hatreds tended to die hard.

6
Damsels in Distress

From the beginning there were subtle, nasty rumors around the Ford White House. *The First Lady was using a number of drugs. Sometimes she used more than one at a time. The First Lady was an addict.* And so on.

"I've seen her so doped she didn't know where she was," one friend was quoted as saying.

The White House staff was well aware of the First Lady's habits, such as staying in bed for hours in the morning and lounging about while everyone else in the place was up and around. Was it true that she was zonked out of her skull half the day?

"She's hell to get up in the morning," one associate admitted.

A newspaper columnist wrote a story to the effect that the First Lady was a very "sick woman" when she first moved into the White House. She was totally dependent on her personal assistant to "get her through the day."

89

The story continued: "She was . . . a 'zombie' who could not get up out of bed, who stayed in a darkened room all day long." In fact, she needed her assistant as a prop, a nursemaid, a nanny, and a keeper. Without help, she was unable to get up, get dressed, or get started on her daily routine.

But that wasn't all. Every evening the First Lady and her assistant had a "happy hour" in the family rooms of the White House. The president, the journalist said, was reportedly very unhappy with his wife's assistant for having cocktails with her.

Other reporters covering the White House were intrigued by the First Lady's deliberately slow and measured pattern of speech. It reminded them of the speech pattern of someone who might be "spaced out," in the jargon of the drug culture. Other observers often commented on her "slurred speech."

A television commentator said that the First Lady used at least three different drugs at one time; her friends were "worried about her" and had no idea where it would all end.

At a going-away party for the secretary of state, the First Lady reportedly was almost totally "out of it."

"It's so nice to see you," the First Lady said to one reporter, in a mechanical, robotlike voice that might have come from outer space. "I'm having such a wonderful time. Doesn't everybody look beautiful? Aren't those pretty dresses?"

"I was stunned," the reporter wrote. "I realized she didn't know who I was, she didn't know where she was, she didn't know who she was."

A drug addict in the White House? An alcoholic? A zonked-out First Lady?

Rumors, rumors, rumors.

However, in the case of Betty Ford, there were more than rumors about her drug addiction and about her drinking habit. But the real story didn't come out while she was in the White House. It came out many months later—in April 1978, while the Gerald R. Fords were moving into their million-dollar "dream house" in Rancho Mirage, near Palm Springs, California.

The mansion had started out as a simple retirement home,

but it had escalated into a marvelous fifteen-room *hacienda* just eleven miles from Palm Springs. In 1978 the Fords were almost a year and a half from the presidency and their residency in the White House.

The former First Lady was writing a book about her early life and her days in the White House, and the former president was working the lecture circuit and preparing his own book about his Washington days.

Betty Ford was in charge of Rancho Mirage, the new house, with her sleeves rolled up and ready to supervise the difficult job of moving the household goods and memorabilia from her earlier residences in Washington.

Because Jerry Ford was on the road, her daughter Susan had come by to help out with the moving. Susan had dropped out of school to take up a career as a professional photographer; she lived in a condominium she had bought in nearby Palm Springs.

In spite of the excitement of moving into the new place, moving was a hard, physically debilitating job. "It's a strain on mother," Susan told an acquaintance. "But she said if [Dad] were around *too* much it would drive her nuts." So, in a way, it was good that Jerry was on the road.

The first days of April 1978 went into unpacking the furniture and boxes of goods sent out from Washington. While Betty was poring over the junk in the crates she found an old packet of Jerry's love letters. When she lifted out the box to take a closer look at them, she felt a twinge of pain, and knew that she had aggravated the pinched nerve in her back.

For fourteen years she had lived with that pinched nerve; it was diagnosed as osteoarthritis—inflammation of the bone and joint. And for fourteen years she had used various drugs to alleviate the pain when it visited her.

Then, of course, she had used other drugs during the two years following her much-publicized mastectomy in September 1974, to fight off any recurrence of cancer. And in 1976 she was pronounced "cured" of the malignancy after two years of exhaustive tests.

Setting aside her husband's love letters, Betty went to the

medicine chest and took one of the prescription drugs she always used to reduce the pain of the osteoarthritis. Then she went to bed.

Her daughter had been with her before during her intermittent bouts of pain, and knew what to expect. But this time Susan noticed that her mother seemed a great deal sleepier and logier than usual.

In the past Betty had sometimes taken one drug to kill the pain from the pinched nerve and another to help her get some sleep. But she had never seemed to be this drowsy before. Susan didn't like her mother's appearance or her inability to function normally. Nor did Betty. Neither one of them had any idea what was wrong.

Jerry Ford was called home from Rochester, New York, where he was scheduled to speak. He flew to Palm Springs. The rest of the Ford family was rounded up as soon as possible.

Mike and his wife, Gayle, came in from Pittsburgh, where they were living afer Mike's graduation from theological school in Massachusetts. Jack drove in from Los Angeles, where he was working as assistant to the publisher of *Outside*, a magazine started by the publisher of *Rolling Stone*. And Steve came over from Newport, California, where he was working for a veterinarian and teaching horseback riding.

It was not an unusual summons. After all, Betty Ford was about to celebrate her birthday on April 8. But the call was a bit ominous. The family found her "tense and anxious."

She admitted that she was worried about certain unusual reactions she was having from the drugs she was taking. After some very plain talk among the members of that plain-talking family it was decided that the First Lady was perhaps "overmedicating" herself with painkilling drugs. In other words, she was for all practical purposes hooked on drugs.

She was counseled by her physician to get treatment for her problem. And it was decided by the president that she should make a complete statement to the public about it, to cover up nothing, and to admit that she was probably addicted to prescription drugs.

By admitting the truth, she might be able to help other women who were going through the same thing, but were afraid to let the truth come to light. "Drug addiction" automatically created a bad image.

Betty Ford was never one to hide ugly facts about herself. As First Lady she had released the full truth about her mastectomy in 1974. It was in character for her to face all kinds of distasteful problems head-on.

Together the former First Lady and president prepared statements for the press—one from her, and one from him. Then they selected a date when she should report to the hospital.

Once she was in Long Beach Naval Hospital undergoing alcohol and drug rehabilitation, her statement was read by one of her husband's aides:

"Over a period of time, I got to the point where I was overmedicating myself. It's an insidious thing, and I mean to rid myself of its damaging effects. There have been too many other things I've overcome to be forever burdened with this."

Her husband's statement said that the treatment she would undergo in the alcohol and drug rehabilitation center was in no way related to her cancer surgery in September 1974. "The cancer has been totally arrested, and her subsequent recovery complete."

Later on there was another statement, this one from a member of the hospital staff. "She had developed a dependence she is trying to overcome," he said, and refused to identify the drugs she had been using or to predict how long she would be hospitalized.

The story hit all the newspapers and electronic media. There were follow-up stories that described her condition in greater detail. Excessive drowsiness was a major contributing factor to her decision to enter the hospital for treatment, one statement said.

The drowsiness was blamed on the combined side effects of the various drugs she was taking under prescription. "She's an active lady and she didn't like [drowsiness] at all," her husband's aide reported. "She can't really raise hell in that condition."

Meanwhile, she was being carefully "demedicated" from the drugs she had been using. Her doctors had already determined that no single drug was responsible for her problem; rather it was "a subtle combination of things." That is, the combined effects of several drugs—one taken for the pinched nerve, another taken to bring on sleep—had been having deleterious effects on her. And she wanted to reduce her dependency on all of them.

"She's undertaken a bold step, typically meeting this problem head-on," the former president's aide reported. "We think she needs a few days to herself."

It was her son Steve who reported that his mother had been taking Valium, a tranquilizer, frequently prescribed both for the treatment of anxiety and as a muscle relaxant. But, he pointed out, there were "several drugs" that she used in combination with Valium. And one of those "several drugs" was alcohol.

"My mother *does* drink," Steve said. "Just as many other people do in this country. There always seems to be a problem mixing alcohol with drugs."

That was news. Alcohol *and* drugs. The revelation caused a few raised eyebrows among friends and associates of Betty Ford, and it caused raised eyebrows among a number of Americans.

Then the rumors of drugs and alcohol during the First Lady's White House days *were* true. Indeed they were. But now, with the story out in the open, there was no need for any more whispers or innuendos.

Meanwhile, there were immediate and positive reactions to Betty Ford's admission to the Long Beach Naval Hospital. She improved rapidly. Within weeks she was back home at Rancho Mirage. And after several return visits, she was finally released permanently. Once again she issued a statement:

"Through the excellent treatment I have had here at the

Long Beach Naval Hospital, I have found I am not only addicted to the medication I have been taking for my arthritis but also to alcohol, so I am grateful for this program of recovery.

"This program is well known throughout the country, and I am pleased to have the opportunity to attend it. I expect this treatment and fellowship to be a solution for my problems and I embrace it not only for me but for all the many others who are here to participate."

One physician followed that up with:

"Her courage in calling the problem what it is will lead to more candor in the way we discuss prescription drugs. By dealing with the problem as it is, she will make it easier for hundreds of people to face the problem much more honestly. Mrs. Ford has made a big contribution—there are hundreds and thousands of other Americans who need this rehabilitation."

Within weeks Betty Ford was fully recovered from her bout with alcoholism and drug addiction. By her courage and openness she was able to face a future without the dread of dissolution and self-destruction.

Ida McKinley was not as lucky as Betty Ford. Although she was not addicted to drugs or alcohol she did have a health problem. Unfortunately, her affliction was not as well understood at the time of her residency in the White House as it is today. Because of that, a veil was thrown over her malady—in the literal as well as the figurative sense.

There were rumors aound the White House, around Washington, around the country—rumors about the First Lady's sanity, about her health, about her mental condition. The rumors were never really corrected or even refuted. In those days medical problems like hers were not discussed in what was termed "polite society"; things not understood were best kept in the dark.

Ida Saxton was one of two daughters of the well-to-do Saxton family of Canton, Ohio. Her sister, Mary, called Pina, was the plain-looking one. Ida was the pretty one, with auburn hair, soft blue eyes, and a pale esthetic complexion. There was a brother, George Saxton, about whom more mention was made in Chapter Five.

Ida Saxton had finished Brooke Hall Seminary for girls at Media, Pennsylvania, along with her sister. Although Ida had been a victim of what her family and family doctor termed "nervousness" as a child, she had seemingly outgrown it and now appeared fit and fashionable.

Her father decided that she should acquire the polish of a businesswoman. So Ida became cashier at her father's bank, the First National of Canton.

When she married William McKinley in 1871, the ceremony was a social milestone in Canton. The couple honeymooned in New York, returned, and set up house in town. They had two children by 1873.

The second birth was a difficult one for Ida. The baby was frail and sickly. Complications ensued for the mother. She developed phlebitis; she had convulsions that may have been epileptic; and she went into severe depression. The baby died.

This affected her relationship with Katie, her first daughter. She would hardly let the girl out of her sight and would clutch her for hours on her lap, weeping in a dark room.

Abner McKinley, her brother-in-law, saw young Katie swinging on the front gate during that gloomy period and asked her to take a walk with him.

"No, I mustn't go out of the yard," Katie told him, "or God'll punish mamma some more."

And apparently that was exactly what happened. Katie died in 1876—the year her father was elected to Congress.

Ida McKinley never fully recovered from the deaths of her daughters. She was an invalid the rest of her life, suffering from a complicated combination of epilepsy, seizures, depression, and self-centered invalidism. The phlebitis had left her a cripple; she walked with difficulty and pain. She was subject to frequent attacks of petit mal—a form of epilepsy characterized by brief losses of consciousness—and to prolonged and violent epileptic seizures. Headaches that were so blinding that she could not think robbed her of the ability to communicate easily.

Her husband never mentioned a word of his wife's problems. He spent most of his life shielding her from the public. Her beautiful face changed under the physical strain. The skin tightened into a twisted mask; her eyes became fearful and sharp, or were dulled by sedatives, of which she took many. She cropped her hair short, saying that the weight of hairpins and braids tormented her.

By the time she became First Lady, Ida McKinley had become quite inured to her role of invalid. Her bouts with hysteria were less frequent, but she was in no way normal.

During the inauguration reception she experienced a sudden attack in the middle of the procession to the ballroom. Instantly the ceremonies halted, and she was gently hustled into the supper room, to vanish for the evening.

The First Lady did not withdraw from her duties as White House hostess, however. Probably she should have, but she was a determined woman.

Because of her debilities the president chose to seat her not at the opposite end of the dining table, but at his right, next to him. There he could shield her more easily from her seizures, facial tics, and other symptoms.

Although it was unpleasant for visitors to be present during one of her attacks, the president or one of Ida McKinley's close relatives would try to screen her from view by holding a napkin or handkerchief in front of her face until the attack had subsided.

Newspapermen and Washington gossips were not actually aware of the extent of her invalidism. During one informal dinner Judge William Howard Taft, later to be twenty-seventh president of the United States, asked the president for a pencil to write something down.

He later reported that he heard "a peculiar hissing sound" from the lips of the First Lady. Slightly shaken, Taft looked up, but saw only that the president had whipped up his napkin from his lap to hold it in front of the First Lady's face, at the same time calmly handing the pencil over to Taft. Taft was astounded at the lack of concern exhibited by the other guests.

The words *epilepsy* and *fit* were never used by the press of the time—friendly or unfriendly. The First Lady was simply described as being in "delicate" health. During his long occupation in the White House, Franklin Delano Roosevelt, unable to stand by himself and always requiring assistance in moving anywhere, was never referred to as a cripple.

The mores of the times did not require, or even desire, the total frankness of today's press, nor would it have ever deemed within the realm of possibility that the public had a right to know.

In Ida McKinley's case, the press cooperated by taking many photographs of her, showing her white face and dreamy, unfocused eyes. The impression of her "charming fragility" aroused great sympathy in the public. She would pose languidly, dressed in lace, in the White House conservatory, a rose in her hand, presenting an image of absolute sublimity. Sometimes she would appear draped in velvet in the Green Room, cooling herself listlessly with a fan.

It was the image she wished to create—the frail and gentle lady, the martyr to the demands of her public position, the wife sweetly resigned to the demands of her beloved husband's career.

One young boy who was brought to the White House by his mother to see the First Lady was being greeted routinely by Ida McKinley when suddenly her face went absolutely rigid. It was as if she was instantly frozen into a statue. A White House relative by her side immediately threw a large silk handkerchief over her head, masking her face from the boy.

"What is it?" the boy cried out in horror. "*What's the matter with her?*"

Almost as quickly as she had stiffened and gone into rigidity the First Lady recovered. The handkerchief came away, and the conversation continued as if it never had been interrupted.

The boy was dazed and a bit frightened, not understanding at all what had happened. His mother whispered to her son that the First Lady simply was "not well."

Sometimes the First Lady would find herself in improved health. "Now she can almost walk alone," was a constant White House remark when she was feeling better. Although most often feeble and lame, subject to headaches, and constantly sinking into little swoons, she did manage to get about. Any agitation, however, would bring on aggravated attacks. Yet she loved to travel with the president.

On a visit to a fashionable resort of Lenox, Massachusetts, the McKinleys were invited to the home of Mr. and Mrs. John Sloane. The Sloanes had borrowed a neighbor's butler, Auguste Chollet, to provide a dinner in honor of the president and First Lady.

Chollet was famous in the area for his most original table decorations. This time he outdid himself with a patriotic display that would never be forgotten.

Chollet worked for days at his creation, which involved a mechanical device connected to a large clock in the cellar of the house. When the president and First Lady entered the dining room they saw a mound covered by a flag in the center of the dining table.

After grace Chollet whisked off the flag, disclosing a real American eagle, dead and stuffed, but suddenly beginning to flap its wings in a robotlike motion. The mechanical bird then winked and nodded at the First Lady.

In horror she tried to get to her feet, stumbled, and almost fell lifeless to the floor. The Sloanes, not really aware of the First Lady's disabilities, had seated her on the opposite side of the table from her husband. McKinley rushed around the table and picked her up from the floor, carrying her half-fainting and moaning from the room.

The clockwork eagle was dumped out on the front lawn.

During the sad affair of George Saxton's murder, Ida tried to rise above it. Yet she and her sister, Pina, were very close to their brother. The First Lady mourned his death and the scandal that surrounded it, in secret. In public she pretended that nothing had happened. Days after her brother's funeral, she was talking to guests in the White House about how much the wild tribes of northern Luzon, in the Philippines, needed missionary help.

"Mrs. McKinley talked ten to the minute about converting the Igorrotes," William C. Beer dryly wrote, deliberately misspelling the tribe's name per her pronunciation. She told him she wanted his children to pray for them. Not one word did she speak about her dead brother.

But her brother's death told on her in a physical way. Within weeks she suffered a severe epileptic attack during a visit to Massachusetts, and went into a hysterical depression as bad as some of the more critical ones she had suffered ten years or more before. She recovered slowly, but was eventually herself again. The First Lady was never, for a moment, out of the president's mind. On the day the battleship *Maine* was sunk in Havana harbor, he was discussing the situation with guests. Suddenly he lifted his head and said, "But I must return to Mrs. McKinley at once. She is among strangers."

His fantastic devotion to her never wavered. Three years later, on September 6, 1901, after being reelected to a second term, President McKinley was assassinated by anarchist Leon Czolgosz. As he fell, he cried to the maddened crowd: "Don't let them hurt him!"

When he could speak again, he whispered: "My wife. Be careful how you tell her—oh, be careful." Always solicitous of her, right up to the end of his life, he died on September 14.

Ida McKinley survived him by six years, dying in 1907 at home in Canton, Ohio.

From the beginning of Mary Todd Lincoln's residence in the White House she was the target of opposition writers and politicians of all stripes. So was her husband, the president.

He expected it; indeed, he rolled with the punches, and enjoyed giving back, blow for blow, every thrust he took. But the First Lady had come from a genteel background. She did not revel in slander. She was hurt by it.

Mary Todd came from Kentucky's affluent bluegrass society. Her father, Robert Smith Todd, was president of a branch of the Bank of Kentucky in Lexington. Her mother, Eliza Parker, was a member of the city's society.

At the age of eight, Mary attended Dr. John Ward's Private Academy, and after finishing up in 1832, she attended Madame Mentelle's, a special school for girls, from fourteen on, where she learned to read, write, and speak French, and where the proper finishing touches were administered to her persona.

Mary was not prepared to be the target of small-minded journalists and snide mainstream politicos. But they were everywhere those days because the Civil War had just begun and tension was stretching everyone's nerves to the breaking point.

Everything was fair game for the Lincoln haters. And because it was difficult to score on Lincoln since he had the wit to turn back insults, they zeroed in on Mary Lincoln. In many instances, they had good cause to. Mary was a headstrong, sophisticated, opinionated, snobbish, intelligent woman, even if she was dignified and ladylike.

Her habit of appearing in low-cut dresses, with shoulders and bodice exposed, caused one visitor to write that "the weakminded Mrs. Lincoln had *her bosom* on exhibition, and a flower pot on her head."

The president himself saw her dressed one night and sighed: "Whew! Our cat has a long tail tonight. Mother, it is my opinion if some of that tail was nearer the head, it would be in better style."

It was Mary's idiosyncrasy not to think much of her husband's speechmaking. And that was made much of by the enemy press. It is not known how she reacted to the Gettysburg Address, which the world acclaimed as a model for speechmaking, but she once was heard to intone after one of his addresses: "That was the worst speech I've ever heard. I wanted the earth to sink and let me through!"

Mary had pinched pennies for so long during her early married years that now she felt she could spend money to decorate the White House and make it at least presentable after its years of austerity. And, of course, when the splendor of the mansion became visible to the public, cries went up that she was wasting money while the "boys fighting the war" were going hungry.

By 1861 she had already exceeded the $20,000 amount Congress had allotted to furnish the White House by some $6,700.

Lincoln learned of the overcharge and was outraged. He could not, in good conscience, approve such an overrun "for flub-dubs for this damned old house," he cried, "when the soldiers cannot have blankets."

When he found it was Mary who was responsible, he threatened to pay the money out of his own pocket. Mary heard about it. He didn't pay for it; it was included in another appropriation for "sundry" expenses.

Almost before she got a chance to accustom herself to life in the White House, the First Lady and the president were devastated by a deep personal loss. They had already suffered one: their second boy, Edward Baker, had died in childbirth. Their oldest boy, Robert Todd, was attending college at the time the Lincolns moved into the White House. Willie, their third boy, was eleven years old just before Christmas in 1861. Tad was the youngest.

Willie fell ill with a raging fever shortly after his birthday. The physicians treating him said that he would be up and around in no time. They were wrong. He never recovered. On February 20, 1862, he died, apparently of typhoid fever.

With the turmoil of the war raging around them, and the increasing intensity of the political attacks on the president and on the First Lady, the death of Willie almost demolished Mary. For weeks and months after his death, she canceled receptions, band concerts, and other entertainments the

Washingtonians had come to expect of the White House hostess.

But eventually, after a year of intense mourning, the White House held a New Year's Day reception in 1863, mostly to celebrate the Emancipation Proclamation. For publicity purposes, Tom Thumb and his bride were guests of honor at the affair.

The political opposition kept getting on Lincoln over the fact that his oldest son Robert was not in uniform but had spent his days on the Harvard University campus living the life of Riley, and even after graduation from the school in 1864 was not in uniform.

Once again it was really Mary Todd Lincoln's fault. The president and the First Lady disagreed completely about Robert's welfare. She wanted him home safe and sound; Lincoln knew that he would be better off serving his country. The president finally wrote to General Ulysses S. Grant in January 1865, asking him if he could find a place for Robert, then twenty-two and a graduate of Harvard, somewhere in the "military family with some nominal rank." He offered to pay the boy himself. "I do not wish to put him in the ranks, nor yet to give him a commission, to which those who have already served long are better entitled, and better qualified to hold."

Grant appointed him a captain and adjutant general, and attached him to his staff. Robert turned out to be a good worker, a solid personality, and very popular with his fellow officers.

This bit of string-pulling was done by a man who hated to seek favors for himself; but Lincoln would do anything for his own kinfolk even under pressure from the opposition. He was forced to listen to criticism of the move for many months before the war ended.

The First Lady loathed General Grant. Having Southern sympathies anyway, she tended to follow rebel estimates of his courage. "He is a butcher," she said, "and is not fit to be at the head of an army."

Lincoln pointed out that Grant was a successful general.

"Yes, he generally manages to claim victory, but such a victory! He loses two men to the enemy's one. He has no management, no regard for life. If the war should continue four years longer, and he should remain in power, he would depopulate the North. Grant, I repeat, is an obstinate fool and a butcher."

Lincoln mused, "Well, Mother, supposing that we give you command of the army. No doubt you would do much better than any general that has been tried."

Mary also had several run-ins with Julia Grant, General Grant's wife. On one occasion the Lincolns and the Grants were taking a river cruise on the *River Queen*, near Grant's headquarters on the James River. When the men rode out from the boat, the women stayed aboard.

Mary was in one of her depressed moods that day. Mrs. Grant sat down next to her on the sofa. Mary, one account said, turned to her, glared, and snapped: "How dare you be seated, until I invite you!"

Julia Grant in her own autobiography had a slightly different version. "On the departure of the gentlemen," she wrote, "Mrs. Lincoln politely pointed to the little sofa from which she had arisen and invited me to be seated. As I was standing near her, I seated myself beside her on this small sofa; then, seeing a look of surprise from Mrs. Lincoln, I immediately started up, exclaiming, 'I crowd you, I fear.' She kindly extended her hand to detain me, saying, 'Not at all.' "

Later, Lincoln, Grant, and Major General Edward O. C. Ord, commanding the Army of the James, were reviewing the troops. Mary and Julia followed in an "ambulance," an open-sided carriage. Because the review was in progress and Mary and Julia had not arrived, Ord's wife, a beautiful woman and excellent horsewoman, was assigned to wait for them.

As time went on, and the ladies still hadn't shown up, Mrs. Ord asked a staff officer if she should accompany the men. He said, "Of course; come along." She took her place in the reviewing column.

When the ambulance approached, Mary saw the woman near the president, almost as if she might be riding at his side. The First Lady had a pathological hatred of any woman who sought to appear at the side of her husband. She was beginning to fume.

An officer galloped up and smiled. "The president's horse is very gallant, Mrs. Lincoln. He insists on riding by the side of Mrs. Ord."

Mary turned red. "What do you mean by that, sir?"

The officer bolted away hastily.

Mrs. Ord turned and saw the ambulance arriving. She galloped up and gave a warm greeting to the First Lady.

Mary had been restraining herself, but now she blew up, calling the rider vile names quite audible to the crowd of officers surrounding her. She finally asked Mrs. Ord what she meant by accompanying the president.

Mrs. Ord said nothing, but burst into tears.

Mary didn't notice and continued to shout and abuse her.

Julia Grant tried to defend the general's wife as best she could. Now Mary turned on her and glowered. All her scathing hatred bubbled to the surface.

"I suppose you think you'll get to the White House yourself, don't you?"

Julia Grant studied Mary Lincoln a moment, and then said rather stolidly that she was quite happy with her own position in life. In fact, she gave the First Lady to understand it was even more than she had ever expected out of life.

Mary turned up her nose. "Oh, you had better take it if you can get it!" she snapped. " 'Tis very nice."

At the time of Lincoln's assassination on April 14, 1865, the First Lady's personal bills added up to an unbelievable $70,000. With her husband's death, Mary had no income of her own—there were no death benefits in those days, nor did Congress appropriate a widow's pension for a murdered president.

The government did pay her the balance of his $25,000 salary for the year 1865. Lincoln's own estate was worth roughly $110,000 when it was settled in 1869—government bonds and real estate in Springfield—but that was divided into three parts for Robert, Tad, and Mary, allowing each of them an income of $1,700 a year from the interest. But it took time to settle the estate.

Her creditors, fearful of ending up with nothing, began hounding her for payment. At first Mary, surrendering to the deep grief of her bereavement, paid no attention to them. But it soon became apparent she would have to pay them off or have the whole story of her extravagances escalate into another full-fledged scandal.

Secretly she and her seamstress, Elizabeth "Lizzie" Keckley, took bundles of her White House clothes and silks to New York to sell. Teetering on the brink of a nervous breakdown, which had always been a potential threat to her, Mary mismanaged the discreet sale, allowed her identity to be ascertained, and became the victim of a bitter press attack on her extravagances and secret dealings in selling her things.

Meanwhile, Robert was engaged to be married to Mary Eunice Harlan, the daughter of Senator James Harlan of Iowa. He came to his mother's rescue. The scandal blew over. She received some money from the sale of the things, but the public wasn't allowed to forget.

"You could hardly believe it possible, but my mother protests to me that she is in actual want and nothing I can do or say will convince her to the contrary," he wrote later in a letter to Mary Harlan. An acquaintance said she had an "insane delusion that poverty stared her in the face."

Robert was married in 1868 and then, as suggested by her son, Mary took Tad for a trip to Europe later the same year.

In Europe Tad went to school in Germany and as he struggled through adolescence, a long-standing speech defect improved until his diction was almost completely normal. Meanwhile, friends in Congress had pushed through a bill for a widow's pension for Mary. Pegged at $5,000 a year, the bill failed the first time through. However, two years later, the pension was approved at $3,000 a year.

Mary and Tad returned to the United States in 1871. Tad had been suffering from colds and fever, and when they arrived in New York, he took a turn for the worse. On June 15, 1871, he died. Once again Mary was devastated by the death of someone close to her. First Eddie, then Willie, then her husband; now Tad.

Her mind seemed to be going. She moved aimlessly from place to place. She began going on mad spending sprees, buying watches, perfumes, trunks, lace curtains, jewelry—all things she had no need for. Robert spent days of his time trying to curb her excesses, with total lack of success. But there was more to the problem than simple extravagance.

When she saw Robert again, late in the spring of 1875, at the Grand Pacific Hotel in Chicago after a trip to Florida, she told him that someone had tried to poison her during breakfast in Jacksonville on the way up. She also said that her pocketbook had been taken from her by a "wandering Jew" in Florida.

On April 1 Mary left her hotel room half-clad and tried to take the elevator down to the hotel lobby. Robert grabbed her and began to steer her back to her room. She became hysterical in the corridor and screamed for help. "You are going to murder me!" Finally he got her back to bed.

The shopping sprees continued during the daytime. She showed Robert securities worth some $57,000, which she always carried on her person. Robert hired a Pinkerton man to watch over her so she wouldn't be robbed. She then decided that someone was following her to harass her!

Things were really getting out of hand. Robert finally decided to have his mother committed to a rest home. Commitment necessitated a trial. The trial, in May 1875, was a sad one, with Mary sitting stunned as her son, pale and red-eyed with weeping, testified against her.

"Oh, Robert, to think that my son would ever have done this!" she sobbed. She wrested her hand away from him when he tried to take it as the jury left the courtroom.

She was adjudged insane and committed to Bellevue Place, a private asylum at Batavia, Illinois. The night before her departure Mary made her way out of the hotel and went to a nearby pharmacist. The pharmacist recognized her and refused to sell her the laudanum she requested.

He followed her to another nearby pharmacy; that pharmacist also refused her request. She tried one more place, where she was given a placebo—a vial falsely labeled laudanum and camphor. At the hotel she drank this down without pause.

Had it been the drug she requested, she would have succeeded in killing herself. There were no further incidents before her admission to Bellevue Place.

Every week Robert visited his mother, frequently taking along her little grandson, Abraham Lincoln. Robert now had three children: Mary, born in 1869; Abraham, 1873; and Jessie, a girl, 1875.

Mary Todd Lincoln's nightmare of commitment did not last long. Her sister, Elizabeth Todd Edwards, had taken an interest in the situation, and had decided that Robert was wrong. The Edwardses managed to have Mary released from the hospital into their custody in September.

Eventually, about a year after the first trial, there was a second; Mary was adjudged sane this time. By now she felt well enough to travel again, and fled to Europe for several years. In Paris she hurt herself in a fall, injuring her spine. In addition to her physical ailments, her mind became shaky once again. She returned to the United States in 1880, after four years abroad. In 1882 she suffered a stroke while living in Springfield and died there.

7

More Beautiful People

Once upon a time there were two sisters. One had beauty and the other had brains.

Although she was younger, the beautiful sister was wed first. Her husband was handsome, well-to-do, and an aristocrat.

The brainy sister was wed shortly afterward. Her husband was a very rich commoner who wanted to be king.

The beautiful sister tired of her handsome groom and got rid of him. She wanted to be wed to a man who could be king, too. She wed a prince in another country and became a princess.

The commoner who wanted to be king did become king, although he was not called king. The brainy sister became queen, although she was not called queen.

The princess sister tired of being a princess and met a rich frog in a far-off land. He was the biggest frog in the pond. But the frog was already married.

The man who would be king was overthrown and the brainy sister became a grieving queen widow. The world fell at her feet, worshipping her for her courage and her style.

The rich frog's wife was carried off by the frog's arch rival and he was alone and sad. To provide solace not only to the rich frog but to the bereaved queen, the princess sister brought the queen to the rich frog's pond.

He gave the queen lavish gifts and took her on a cruise of his pond to exorcise her grief.

An evil sorcerer threw magic dust in the bereaved queen's eyes and she fell in love with the frog, thinking him a rich and famous shipping magnate.

The frog and the brainy sister were wed, but the sorcerer ran out of magic dust. On the morning after her wedding night, the queen awoke to find herself in bed with a frog.

When the brainy sister's adoring subjects saw their queen in bed with a frog, they turned against her. But when the frog died and his wife returned to her native land, they bowed down in the streets to her and followed her everywhere she went.

The beautiful sister tired of her prince and allowed herself to be carried off by a commoner. She too returned to her native land and became a dancing girl and a mime.

And the subjects worshipped them both as Beautiful People to the end of their days.

MORAL: You don't need to be beautiful to be one of the Beautiful People. You don't need to be brainy to make a damned fool of yourself. And you don't need to be either to be the most noticed woman of the twentieth century—but it helps.

Jacqueline Lee Bouvier was married to John Fitzgerald Kennedy on September 12, 1953, over a hundred years after Mary Todd married Abraham Lincoln—but there were similarities in their emotional makeup that caused their White House days to be markedly similar.

Both women had stepparents who caused some dissonance in their psychological profiles. Both women went on shopping sprees and overspent their budgets enough to cause their husbands to roar with rage. Both women were widowed by the bullets of assassins in their prime years.

In many ways the Kennedy-Bouvier nuptials was an ideal media marriage—the union of a charming, aloof, and smart young woman of a good social background and a dashing, charismatic, scrapping politician who had the advantage of money and grit instead of background.

The Bouvier family was rent by a divorce and remarriage, but was a combination, from the beginning, of social-climbing and blueblood stock. The Kennedy family was a closely knit, active, and overpoweringly aggressive bunch.

Jacqueline's father, who divorced her mother when Jacqueline was a young girl, was a true playboy of the early 1920s. Called "Black Jack" Bouvier for his swarthy and handsome image, he did all the things playboys should do with the possible exception of making money easily.

His virility, it was said in his younger days, tended to attract both sexes. Whispers went about that he was a switch-hitter; that he had been intimate with Cole Porter, who graduated with him from Yale University in 1914.

"I'm just mad about Jack," Porter had told friends.

Black Jack had an uncanny resemblance to Clark Gable, who became the heartthrob of the nation's women in the 1930s and '40s. When he was mistaken for Gable, Bouvier did not gnash his teeth in rage.

Jacqueline's divorced mother, Janet Lee Bouvier, did not stay unmarried long. Her second husband was Hugh D. Auchincloss. "Hughdie" Auchincloss had wads of money. Bouvier, who was beginning to lose his ability to make any money at all, was green-eyed jealous of Auchincloss and his ability to live high. Most of Jacqueline's early life involved struggles between the Auchincloss and Bouvier factions for her fealty and love.

Jacqueline's younger sister, Caroline Lee Bouvier, was prettier and more feminine than she was. Jacqueline had brains and Lee—never called Caroline—beauty. Jacqueline's ego was frequently shattered by comparisons made between them by family friends.

She was a straight-A student throughout her youth. She learned quite early to submerge her obvious intelligence in such a fashion that it did not make other people jealous or antagonistic. After finishing at Miss Porter's school in Farmington, she enrolled at Vassar, took a year off in Paris on a Smith College exchange course to study at the Sorbonne in Paris, and then graduated from George Washington University in Washington.

In 1950, the year of her graduation, Jacqueline was engaged, but for only a short time. She got a job on the *Washington Times-Herald* as the "Inquiring Camera Girl," through contacts that went like this: Hugh D. Auchincloss mentioned her to his friend Arthur Krock of the *New York Times* Washington bureau, who mentioned her to his friend Frank Waldrop of the *Washington Times-Herald,* who mentioned her . . .

It was in this job that she met Senator John F. Kennedy, a rising star on the political horizon, straining at the leash, to mix metaphors, for national prominence.

Jacqueline's sister Lee beat her out in the marriage sweepstakes, as she had always beat her out in the beauty derby. Lee was married in 1952 to Michael Canfield, son of Cass Canfield, top editor at Harper Brothers in New York.

Sibling rivalry was a submerged thing in the Bouvier girls, but it was very real. Evidence of rivalry surfaced immediately. Within two months Jacqueline was engaged to John F. Kennedy. They were married less than a year later.

"Jackie was motivated by money," said Nancy Dickerson, a television commentator. "Though she grew up in the midst of luxury, extravagant amounts were not spent on her, and early on she had vowed to marry someone 'richer than Uncle Hughdie,' her stepfather."

Whatever the motivation, Jacqueline married one of the capital's most dashing young Lochinvars. The announcement of their engagement was held up until the *Saturday Evening Post* had run an article in June 1953, titled "Jack Kennedy—the Senate's Gay Young Bachelor."

Black Jack Bouvier was on the skids now; he had been going down since the Depression. When Lee was married, he gave away his daughter; Jacqueline asked him to give her away. But by now a confirmed alcoholic, he failed to appear at the wedding; he was dead drunk in a nearby hotel. His bitter rival, Hugh D. Auchincloss, gave her away.

The story went that Janet Auchincloss saw to it that "friends" plied her ex-husband with liquor the night before and deliberately got him so drunk he couldn't attend.

Black Jack was hustled back to New York and locked himself in his hotel room for days, refusing to speak to anyone.

The newlyweds settled into their marriage somewhat tentatively, with Jack Kennedy continuing to lead his busy political and social life, and Jacqueline not changing her own life-style much except to quit her newspaper job.

She discovered immediately that the magazine stories and the gossips were right: Her husband was indeed a womanizer, and was not about to quit the habit. In the ensuing months, the married couple were frequently apart—Jack on trips here and there, and Jacqueline dating friends from her past or reading in solitary.

In Washington the word went out that Jack was sleeping around as much as he had before he slipped on the matrimonial halter.

It wasn't only her husband's sex life that bothered Jacqueline. She had to contend with the whole Kennedy clan. They all seemed overbearingly aggressive, especially Jack's sisters.

"They were always talking about how much money they had, how influential Joe was, and how much power the family possessed," said Senator George Smathers. "They'd drive you crazy with that kind of talk. . . . I think it really got to Jackie after a while."

She became the victim of black moods—the kind of depressive moods a person of sensitivity who read a great deal and kept to herself the way Jackie did *would* experience. One physical manifestation of those moods was her habit of biting her fingernails. Her nails were so stubby and bleeding that she refused ever to wear nail polish; it would call attention to her mangled fingertips.

"There was something quite remote in her," Norman Mailer wrote, "not willed, not chilly, not directed to anyone in particular but distant, detached as psychologists say, moody and abstracted the novelists used to say. . . . She had perhaps a touch of that artful madness which suggests future drama."

Outwardly composed and almost icy, she was inwardly a seething mass of conflicting emotions. Her inner struggles caused by her mother pulling her in one direction and her father in another had scarred her psyche permanently.

In her married years, Jacqueline Kennedy had two miscarriages, and bore three children, one of whom died within days. For a Kennedy, this was obviously not enough. Jacqueline could not help but feel inadequate in her role as the wife of Jack Kennedy.

At one time during their years together, Jacqueline tried to fight her recurring moods of depression with a stay at Valleyhead, a private psychiatric clinic in Carlisle, Massachusetts. Carlisle specialized in electroshock therapy. Because of the possible political implications of this type of therapeutic treatment, the fact was kept secret.

Truman Capote remembered her from her student years at Farmington. "I don't know what is wrong with Jackie," he said, "except that she is way out in orbit somewhere."

Another friend put it this way: "I don't think she was born happy."

Once in the White House, Jacqueline's problems did not

lessen. Jack, womanizing more than ever, now openly brought some of his women into the White House, particularly when his wife was out of town.

The First Lady found a woman's panties tucked in a pillowcase in her husband's room one time. She held it out to him, saying in that small-girl voice of hers: "Would you please shop around and see who these belong to? They're not my size."

There were stories about the president's private parties, in which women ran around naked, jumping into and out of the swimming pool, and then prancing through the White House hallways.

"Just as the elevator door opened," one White House worker said, "a naked blonde office girl ran through the hall. Her breasts were swinging as she ran by. There was nothing to do but for me to get out fast and push the button for the basement."

Jacqueline Kennedy, the story went, was ready to divorce Jack as soon as their White House years ended.

Money, which had always been an important factor in the life of Jacqueline Bouvier, became even more important in the president's mansion, as it was important in the lives of many other First Ladies, including Mary Todd Lincoln.

During the first year the Kennedys were in the White House, Jacqueline's expenses for clothing, art, food and liquor, medical, jewelry, beauty salon, and gifts totaled a staggering $105,446.14!

"Do you realize I only make $100,000 a year as president?" Jack Kennedy shouted at her when he learned of her bills. "If we didn't have a private income, we'd be bankrupt."

Actually, Kennedy had been giving his salary to charity ever since he had entered Congress in 1947, and he continued to do so as president.

Jacqueline had her own ideas about that. "I could sure use that money myself, Jack."

Kennedy had spent $13 million to finance his election. "I don't understand it," Jacqueline sighed. "Jack will spend any amount of money to buy votes but he balks at investing a thousand dollars in a beautiful painting!"

In 1963 Jacqueline had her third child, a boy, named Patrick. He died within days. The First Lady was shattered. Keeping Caroline and John in the White House, the president sent his wife off on a convalescent cruise.

Jacqueline's sister, Lee, was now married to Prince Stanislaus Radziwill, a bona fide member of European nobility. Princess Lee was a member in good standing of the international jet set, so-called because they flew by jet from one big blowout to another—a kind of permanent movable feast. A rich Greek shipping magnate named Aristotle Onassis loved to host jet set cruises for the Beautiful People. A short, stocky peasant-type himself, he liked to surround himself with Untouchables.

It was Princess Lee who suggested that Jacqueline come along with her on a cruise aboard the Onassis yacht. Actually, Jack Kennedy didn't think much of the idea—Onassis was in some trouble with the United States government and had a bad name among American financiers—but he knew he had to be good to his wife at this particular time.

For "front"—what gossip columnists used to call the "beard"—the Franklin Delano Roosevelt, Jrs., went along with the First Lady. Onassis lavished all kinds of gifts on his guests, but Jacqueline's were the most lavish in memory. When she returned to the United States, the hurt was still there, but dripping in diamonds the First lady was feeling much better.

Although the cruise was not reported in the press as much as the president's daily activities, Jacqueline Kennedy was becoming a star in her own right. Much of her big-name quality dated from her television tour of the White House in 1962, hosted by Charles Collingwood of CBS. The guided tour was witnessed by 46 million Americans as the First Lady wandered through the White House describing gifts and dropping the names of private donors.

"The voice was a quiet parody of the sort of voice one hears on the radio late at night, dropped softly into the ear by girls who sell soft mattresses, depilatories, or creams to brighten the skin," Norman Mailer wrote in a review in *Esquire*.

He thought the show itself was "silly, ill-advised, pointless, empty, dull and obsequious to the most slavish tastes in American life."

"Television at its best," cooed the friendly *Chicago Daily News*.

By now Jacqueline Kennedy had a nickname—Jackie—and it had caught on with a vengeance. There was from that day on only one Jackie in world history. And she was it.

After the tragedy of Patrick's death, she was the number-one name in the news. The stage was set for an even bigger role for her to play—that of the grieving widow. And on November 22, 1963, the curtain went up when an assassin's bullet cut down Jack Kennedy and made Lyndon B. Johnson president.

The First Lady—she was now First Bereaved—stood the test with the super will she had long possessed. Head up, chin in, eyes front, she played the next few days without faltering and became the supreme token of sympathy the world over.

As the human race paid homage to her courage, dignity and nobility, she remained in the central focus of all media coverage. Afterward . . .

She fled Washington finally, moving to New York with her daughter, Caroline, and her son, John. The Kennedys, whom she had long detested, came through for her in her—and their—grief. Her protector became Robert F. Kennedy, and in the rather messy negotiations on the suppression of the William Manchester book about Kennedy's death, he stood firm and became her champion.

Her own image came out of that confrontation somewhat tarnished. The money, it seemed, was what bothered her. Why should Manchester make such a lot of cash just by writing the book? She had *lived* through it, and had got nothing.

Money was the root of her dissatisfaction. The world assumed she had inherited a pot from her husband on his death. But it came to a lump sum of $25,000, plus his personal effects, plus $43,229.26 (his navy retirement pay and allowance, his salary, and his death benefits). So she received less than $70,000 in capital. However, out of the two Kennedy trust funds established for her and the children, her share as widow was an income of about $200,000 a year.

Not bad for anybody else—but this was a woman who was used to blowing $100,000 a year on clothing alone!

Then came another blow: the death by assassination of the man she had come to lean on the most, Robert F. Kennedy. The former First Lady had lost her main supports in life. She needed help from someone else.

That someone else turned out to be Aristotle Onassis. Only four months after her brother-in-law was murdered, Jacqueline Lee Bouvier Kennedy became Jacqueline Lee Bouvier Kennedy Onassis on the island of Skorpios in the fabled Aegean Sea, owned by the man she was marrying.

Pandemonium in the media!

The *Stockholm Expressen:* "JACKIE, HOW COULD YOU?"

Verdens Gang in Oslo: "SHE'S NO LONGER A SAINT!"

The supersaint indeed had feet of clay.

History has recorded few such swings in status from the absolute zenith to the absolute nadir. Overnight the saint had become the sinner.

Such a fall from absolute favor to absolute disfavor should have caused the press to desert her and her public to turn its face from her forever. In point of fact, she became even more photographed, more written about, more featured on the covers of the low-brow magazines that plastered the newsstands.

Several photographers made her image their life's work. Among them was Ron Galella, who began taking candid pictures of her from all angles whenever she was out in public. His concentration on her became an obsession—he sold over 4,000 pictures of her within the span of a few years.

In 1969 Galella was waiting in Central Park when Jacqueline Onassis appeared with her son John Kennedy. Seeing him immediately, she called to her Secret Service escorts, ordering them to seize his film. Galella was manhandled and forced to surrender it; he threatened to take court action.

Jackie had her attorneys bring charges against the photographer for harassment, and Galella had to appear in court to clear himself. He was told to stay at least 150 feet away from her and at least 225 feet away from either her daughter or her son. Four years later the courts became more lenient; the distance was changed to 25 feet for Jacqueline and 30 feet for the children. Time, perhaps, had made them all less photogenic.

Even as Mrs. Onassis, the former First Lady continued her prodigious shopping sprees—sprees which Onassis at first put up with tolerantly, but soon tired of and started to complain about exactly the way Jack Kennedy had.

Jackie's income from the Kennedy estate had stopped when she married Onassis; so had her widow's pension from the U.S. government. All she had was a charge account with Olympic Airlines, which Onassis then owned.

The Onassis marriage was unstable from the beginning. But when Onassis's son, Alexander, died in a helicopter crash, the Jackie-Ari relationship deteriorated completely. Partially it was due to Onassis's health. He was suffering from myasthenia gravis, a degenerative muscle disease, and was rapidly going downhill.

Combined with the death of his son, his ill health made him short-tempered and hard to get along with. His wife's obsessive shopping habits irritated him. During a flight to Acapulco in 1974, he decided to deprive Jacqueline of the quarter of his estate she would be entitled to as a Greek widow.

The way he did it was typical of his Byzantine approach to life. He had the Greek government *change the marriage laws* to eliminate "foreign" wives from the one-quarter provision they were traditionally entitled to. Prior to this change, of his nearly half-a-billion-dollar fortune, she could expect about $125 million, maybe even more.

Without telling her about his string-pulling in Athens, he had his wife sign an amendment to their original marriage agreement stipulating that she accept on his death $200,000 a year for life, plus $25,000 a year for each of her children until they were adults.

Jackie signed the amendment, assuming the amount was in addition to the one-quarter of his fortune she would get as his widow; how could she even guess what he was up to—and just to spite her!

At the same time Onassis contacted a New York lawyer to see if some means could be devised whereby he could divorce her. But before any action could be taken, Onassis fell gravely ill and was confined to bed. He died in March 1975.

At his bedside when he died was his daughter Christina, but not his wife. Jackie was in New York. When she discovered that her husband had cut her out of what she considered to be her rightful share of his estate, she was stunned.

For months she and Christina fought over the estate. Their contests made headlines and sold plenty of papers. Eventually, she settled for $26 million. And so Jacqueline Lee Bouvier Kennedy Onassis came out of it richer as a widow than she had been as a wife.

Meanwhile, her sister, Lee, had separated from her husband, the prince. She was in New York, studying interior decorating, then trying out the Broadway stage, and even appearing on television.

The former First Lady and former wife of a rich Greek peasant settled in New York. Could there be anything she could hope to do to top her already fabulous career?

Apparently her public thought so. They continued avid as ever for news about her, for news about her growing daughter, Caroline, and her son, John. But mostly about *her*. They wanted to know whom she was dating. They wanted to know where she was vacationing. They wanted to know what she ate for dinner.

This daughter of a playboy and a social climber, this widow of an adored and short-lived president, this widow of a Greek multimillionaire peasant—this astoundingly intricate and bedeviled person named Jacqueline Bouvier Kennedy Onassis—had become the most famous individual of the twentieth century.

Unlike Jackie Kennedy, who sat at the side of her husband while he died, this First Lady saw her own husband die in a vivid dream that foretold the future with incredible and ghastly accuracy!

To start at the end:

It was a vivid dream, and a very real one. In it Julia Gardiner Tyler saw her husband directly in front of her, deathly pale, holding his collar and tie in his hand. Then she saw him in bed at the Exchange Hotel in Richmond, breathing his last. She was miles away, at home in Sherwood Forest, their estate in eastern Virginia.

The dream was exceptionally *real*. It portended evil. It foretold death. Death again.

Death had played strange tricks on Julia. Death had brought her to marriage. Two deaths, actually: the death of the country's First Lady, and the grisly, unexpected death of her own father.

Now she was seeing a third death—the death of her husband, the father of her seven children.

She took her small baby Pearl and the baby's nurse and drove down to the river to buy passage on a boat to Richmond. She must find her husband to assure herself that he was all right. Yet she knew in her heart that he was *not* all right.

Was she a true clairvoyant? Was she possessed of extrasensory perception, as she thought? Could she read the future? Or was she simply a little bit crazy?

Neither, perhaps; or both.

But then, she had always been *different*. It was her charm, and her cross to bear. Julia Gardiner had been the belle of

New York and Paris, a superstar in the world of society, a bright, sparkling personality in her own right; in truth, a woman fit for the highest position in the land—the perfect First Lady even before she ever thought she might be.

One reporter wrote: "Julia had large gray eyes, raven hair, and the clearest olive complexion, and seemed to attract the most eminent men from the time she entered society."

Another said that she was "a very beautiful and elegantly formed young woman."

Julia was first and foremost an aristocrat, but from a world far removed from the magnolia-scented, languid *beau monde* of the Old South, the society that had produced Letitia Christian, the first Mrs. John Tyler. Julia came from Gardiner's Island—named for her own family—off the eastern extremity of Long Island. Her father, David Gardiner, one-time New York State senator, was a Yale-trained lawyer of impeccable lineage and of the highest social standing. And rich, rich, rich.

On a tour of Europe with her sister, Margaret, mother, and father, Julia was wined and dined by royalty in every country visited. But she was known to the common folk as well as to the leaders of society.

Featured on one colored lithographed throwaway, Julia Gardiner was called "The Rose of Long Island." In the advertising picture, she was dressed in the flamboyant drygoods of a firm called Bogert and Mecamly: heavy fur-hemmed winter coat, and sunbonnet trailing large ostrich feathers. "I'll purchase at Bogert and Mecamly's, No. 86 Ninth Avenue," read the words on a sign she was carrying. "Their goods are beautiful and astonishingly cheap."

Needless to say the Gardiners were piqued by Julia's insensitivity. But it all passed over. The rich and respected could get away with anything. Julia Gardiner met the president of the United States in January 1842, during a White House reception. President John Tyler was happily married to Letitia Christian at the time, and he had a flourishing family of seven children. Then, quite suddenly, in 1842, the very southern First Lady died.

Next time Julia Gardiner returned to see the president, he was a grieving widower. It was December 1842, and Julia and her sister were invited in for a "quiet whist game" by Priscilla Tyler, the president's daughter, who had taken up sojourn in the White House to act as her father's hostess in place of her late mother.

Soon Julia was visiting regularly, sometimes with her sister, sometimes with her father. In February, Tyler began taking notice of her, too, teasing her about her numerous beaux, one of whom was Tyler's own son John, who had separated from his wife and was constantly in and about the White House.

Tyler then attended church with the Gardiners. Their intimacy increased—card games, dances, tête-à-têtes. When Tyler finally proposed marriage to her, Julia refused, but she refused in such a way that the rejection was not an irrevocable one.

By February 1844, the Gardiners were once again at the White House attending various social events, including an outing the president was taking on the Potomac on the steam frigate *Princeton,* on February 25.

As the ship passed Mount Vernon, a newly designed deck cannon was made ready to fire a salute in honor of the president. Something about the cannon was flawed. A tragic explosion occurred. Eight men were massacred on the deck of the ship, and lay in pools of their own blood. Included in the death toll were both the secretaries of state and navy—*and* socialite David Gardiner.

Julia had been below deck when the blast occurred, but she was not hurt. However, when the smoke had cleared away, she found her father, and stood over his body almost hysterical and about to faint.

The president had not been on deck, but was mounting the ladder onto it at the time of the explosion. He rushed forward to find Julia near her father's body, sobbing brokenly. He grabbed her and carried her to safety. Both she and her sister were then taken to the White House to recover from the ordeal.

A White House funeral was held for all the dead. The Gardiners returned to East Hampton to their home.

That was the second death in the strange series. Julia was not known to be superstitious. But she knew now that death was foreordained. Within seven weeks of her father's death, she told Tyler that she would marry him.

It was obvious to those close to the president that something unusual was going on. Tyler's son John was in on the secret. But not the rest of the country. And so it was a tremendous surprise when on the morning of June 26, 1844, the bereaved president of the United States entered the Church of the Ascension on Lower Fifth Avenue, New York, to be married to the recently bereaved Julia Gardiner. John Tyler, Jr. acted as his father's best man. He was fifty-four, she was twenty-four.

Sensation in the press!

The new, dazzling First Lady moved into the White House immediately. For eight months, the windup of Tyler's presidency, the White House bounced and quivered as it had not done since the days of Dolley Madison. The First Lady's wardrobe was as extravagant and sensational as her marriage.

She would receive guests seated on a raised platform—quite like royalty—in front of the south windows of the Blue Parlor. There she would bow regally to guests. But she was so chatty and friendly that her excessive egoism was discounted by her admirers.

Tyler was defeated for reelection by James K. Polk. During his service in Washington, he had purchased an estate in Charles City County, Virginia, called Sherwood Forest. After leaving the White House in 1845, he and Julia moved to Virginia.

There she bore him seven children between the years 1846 and 1860. Their last-born was Pearl. Although she had been born in the North, Julia aligned herself with her husband as the Civil War approached.

Tyler was a leader in an ill-fated peace convention held in Washington in February 1861. As the Southern states began seceding, Tyler participated in the creation of the Southern Confederacy, and was elected to the Confederate House of Representatives.

In 1862 he left Sherwood Forest to attend a state secession convention in Richmond. It was during that time that Julia awoke in the night after seeing the haggard and death-ridden face of her husband in the vivid dream previously mentioned.

Once off the riverboat in Richmond, she hurried to the hotel where her husband was staying, and to her relief found him in excellent health. She was embarrassed; her foreboding of death had been nothing more than an overactive imagination. She never told him what she had seen, but pretended that she had simply become lonely and had traveled up the river to be with him.

Tyler saw no reason to question her for her devotion. The next morning he went downstairs for breakfast before his wife rose. She was in the bedroom upstairs, tending to Pearl. There was a sudden commotion downstairs, and a few moments later the door to her room opened.

There stood John Tyler, deathly pale, collar and tie held in his hand, looking exactly the way he had appeared to her in her dream!

He was deathly ill, having suffered a heart attack. He was put to bed for Julia to attend. On the night of January 17 she awoke and heard him having difficulty breathing. The vascular thrombosis he had suffered had paralyzed his respiratory centers.

Julia got the doctor.

"Doctor, I am going," Tyler sighed.

Julia tried to force brandy into his mouth, but his teeth chattered on the glass. He smiled at her and died.

"It was exactly like the bed I saw him upon in my dream, and unlike any of our own!" Julia wrote later.

Her dream had been a perfect example of precognition. She was apparently the only First Lady blessed—or cursed—with what we now call ESP.

* * *

Rachel Jackson was the only First Lady-elect—that is, she was alive at the time her husband, Andrew Jackson, was elected to the presidency—who died before her husband was able to take the oath of office. Nevertheless, she was so much a part of President Andrew Jackson that even though she was gone she seemed to be standing by his side throughout his years in the White House.

Her influence on him was monumental. His love for her was so strong that he never for one instant forgot her throughout his years in Washington. During his life leading to the presidency she was constantly at his side; for her he dared his life several times, fought duels over her honor, and loved her to the fullest.

She was the epitome of the American frontierswoman. Judged by the standards of her time she was an eccentric, a woman immersed in religion until she was almost a fanatic. But she was an original.

Oddly enough, her background was *not* that of the typical frontierswoman. She came from a prestigious Maryland family headed by Colonel John Donelson. Her great-uncle was the first president of Princeton University, and her father served three terms in the Virginia House of Burgesses.

But financial reversals forced the Donelson family to move westward to the Cumberland River. And that was where Rachel Donelson grew up. It was wilderness country, in the most physical sense of the term; Indian forays occurred sporadically. There were usually shortages of food and bullets.

Rachel grew up to be a good-looking, lusty, and spirited young woman. She was "of medium height, beautifully molded form, full red lips, a glowing olive oval face, rippling with smiles and dimples." And as was the fashion among many frontierswomen of the late nineteenth century, Rachel had a habit of smoking a clay pipe.

At seventeen Rachel met Captain Lewis Robards, the son of a well-to-do Kentucky family. They were married in 1785 and went to live with the Robardses.

These were early settlers, with free-and-easy manners.

They held dances in blockhouses where men drank whiskey directly from the barrel. Rachel Donelson was an excellent dancer. The trouble was, Robards was inordinately jealous of his wife.

Frontier custom decreed that unattached males should be lodged with families for added protection in case of Indian attack. A lawyer named Peyton Short was billeted with the Robardses. Robards was soon accusing his wife of making love to Short, but his mother claimed that it was not true. Nevertheless, the infuriated Robards threw Rachel out of the house four years after they were married. She went back to her widowed mother's place outside Nashville, which was now operating as a boarding house. Two men were living there at the time: John Overton, a lawyer, and Andrew Jackson, then prosecuting attorney for the Western District of North Carolina (later Tennessee).

Soon Robards had a change of heart. He wanted his wife to return to him. She agreed. Robards purchased a farm near the boarding house. For two more years they lived together, with Robards becoming increasingly jealous of Rachel's many male admirers.

There were nasty squabbles. Robards zeroed in on Jackson as his primary rival for Rachel's love. Jackson, always the hothead, challenged him to a duel; Robards backed down. In desperation, Rachel fled to Jackson, asking his help in leaving her husband for good. Jackson escorted her to the home of her sister, Jane Hays, outside Nashville.

Robards then filed a divorce petition in Kentucky. The papers, unknown to Rachel or Jackson, charged that "Rachel Robards did on the——day of July 1790, elope from her husband, said Lewis Robards, with another man." The court denied the petition, but granted Robards the right to sue once again.

Robards soon changed his mind and came crawling back to Rachel. Jackson ordered him off. Robards blamed Jackson for his wife's alienation, and said so in public. Jackson found him.

"If you ever again associate my name with your wife's I'll cut off your ears—I'm tempted to do it anyhow."

In October 1790 Jackson bought a piece of plantation property near Natchez, at Bayou Pierre, where he built a log house. When he returned to Nashville six months later, Robards was in action once again, threatening to carry his wife back to Kentucky.

Rachel was thoroughly frightened and wanted to get as far away from him as possible. Colonel John Stark, an old friend of the Donelson family, offered to take her on a 2,000-mile journey down the Cumberland, the Ohio, and the Mississippi, to Natchez.

Jackson at first tried to persuade her not to make the trip, but she insisted. At the last minute, Jackson was urged to join the flatboat flotilla, and did so.

In Natchez Rachel was put up at the plantation home of Mr. and Mrs. Abner Green, two of Jackson's friends. Jackson then made the trip back to Nashville to find Rachel's mother in despair. Robards had petitioned for divorce on grounds of desertion!

Oddly enough, Jackson, instead of stalking down Robards and facing him, which would have been more in character, asked Rachel's mother if he could marry Rachel.

"Mr. Jackson, would you sacrifice your life to save my poor child's good name?"

Jackson, striking a dramatic pose, replied, "Ten thousand lives, Madam, if I had them."

He then left for Natchez and married Rachel in October 1791. Within months he had bought a riverfront farm near Nashville, from Rachel's brother John Donelson, and the bride and groom settled down there.

In December 1793 the Jacksons were shocked to hear that Robards was once again suing for divorce on the grounds that his wife was living openly with another man; this divorce was promptly granted. Jackson was stunned. He had made a fundamental error; he had assumed, with all the others, that the original divorce petition had gone through. But it had *not*. As a lawyer, he understood the magnitude of his carelessness—their marriage was invalid!

As soon as possible, in January 1794, he and Rachel were married a second time, in a private ceremony, a little less than two years after their first wedding ceremony. But the fact that they had been living together in a state of technical adultery—bigamy for Rachel—for over two years could not be erased by a second marriage. Nor could it be erased by wishing it had not happened.

The news got out. Robards helped spread the word as widely as he could. Talk of Rachel Jackson's bigamy caused her husband to fight a duel with John Sevier, the governor of Tennessee.

Jackson's rise in politics made him enemies as well as friends. There had always been bad blood between Jackson and John Sevier over Jackson's election as major general in the Tennessee militia. Sevier had also been involved in some unsavory land speculations that Jackson had uncovered and publicized. In October 1803, Jackson, now a judge, and Sevier ran into each other in front of the courthouse in Knoxville.

Sevier opened the assault by blaming Jackson for humiliating him. Who did Jackson think he was? Sevier sniped at Jackson for his "pretensions."

Jackson responded by pointing out his victories over the Indians. "I've performed some public services myself, which I believe have met with approval!"

"Services?" Sevier sneered. "I know of no great service you have rendered the country, except taking a trip to Natchez with another man's wife." He pulled his saber.

Jackson turned white. Then he blew up. "Great God!" he thundered. "Do you mention *her* sacred name?" He swung his walking stick at Sevier's hand.

Both men drew pistols. Crowds in the streets scattered. One bystander was grazed by a bullet. But neither antagonist hit the other.

The next day, in a letter, Jackson challenged Sevier to a duel.

"Know ye that I, Andrew Jackson, do pronounce, publish, and declare to the world, that his excellency John Sevier . . . is a base coward and poltroon. He will basely insult, but has not the courage to repair. ANDREW JACKSON. You may prevent the insertion of the above by meeting me in two hours after receipt of this."

Sevier delayed twenty-four hours, and then accepted the challenge.

"I have a friend to attend me. I shall not receive another letter from you, as I deem you a coward."

They met on a road outside Knoxville on the way to the rendezvous point. Jackson drew a pistol, dismounted, and drew a second pistol. Sevier leaped from his horse, a pistol in each hand. "Damn you, Jackson! Fire away!" Each man began loudly cursing the other in the flowery rodomontade of the era. Apparently satisfied, they both put away their pistols.

But then Jackson lunged at Sevier, threatening to cane him. Sevier drew his saber. The governor's horse bolted, carrying the governor's pistols. Jackson drew his pistol, and Sevier ducked behind a tree. "Damn you, Jackson, will you fire on a naked man?" Sevier's seventeen-year-old son, who was his second, drew on Jackson. Dr. Van Dyke, Jackson's second, drew on the son. No one fired. The whole thing had become a mad tableau.

Then, quite suddenly, the tension broke. Everyone began rushing forward making friendly signs. The two men, still cursing and abusing each other verbally, put away their weapons and agreed to end the feud.

The talk of bigamy bothered Rachel Jackson more than it bothered her husband, if that could be possible. She thought that her illegal marriage was more than a simple technicality; she construed it as being sinful. And her sin, she reasoned, was what prevented her from having children. Because she did not become pregnant, Rachel decided that her barrenness was the punishment of God. She took up religion with an almost fanatical fervor.

Never a temperate or even-minded woman, she plunged into her religiosity with an intensity that was frightening. But no matter how much she prayed for forgiveness, she never had any children.

As the years wore on, her husband found himself a folk hero after his long battle with the Cherokee and Creek Indians in Florida. In 1828 he was nominated for the presidency. And the campaign brought Rachel Jackson once again into the spotlight.

Jackson's enemies knew how to handle him. They knew that they could get to him through his wife. And once again the facts about the unfortunate legal complication surrounding the Jackson marriage came out in the newspapers. The story of what had happened over thirty years before became common gossip once again.

Rachel was past sixty now; she was unhappy about the turmoil. It took its toll on her health. She began to brood over what people were saying about her. Her strong faith in God did not help much. She felt guilt over her own actions, considering them sinful in the eyes of the Lord.

Jackson knew that his wife was extremely sensitive about the mix-up over her divorce and remarriage, and he tried to point out to her that her inability to have children was not her fault at all. The more he tried to assuage her, the more upset she became. Jackson knew that the best thing he could do would be to keep her from reading the newspapers and from hearing what people were saying about her.

Rachel was never a very avid reader of the newspapers. Jackson kept most of the widespread gossip from her ears by keeping her among her friends. But outside the house and outside the circle of Jackson's immediate family and close friends the scandal assumed the proportions of a minor hurricane.

Everyone was talking about Rachel's bigamy.

Rachel did not particularly care if her husband won the election or not; in fact, if she had her way, they should both settle down at home.

However, because she was a good wife, she let him go on his political way, campaigning for the highest office in the land. Thus, when he won it, in spite of the talk against him and in spite of the scandal of his marriage, she simply accepted it in the spirit she thought was right.

"For Mr. Jackson's sake," she said, "I am glad. For my own part I never wished it."

At first she would not even join in on the celebrations. But finally she consented to go to Washington with him for the inauguration and live in the White House as the First Lady.

But she made it quite evident what she thought about the presidency in relation to God:

"I had rather be a doorkeeper in the house of God than to live in that palace."

Having made up her mind to go to Washington, Rachel then went out to shop for a wardrobe in Nashville. Even after her husband's election, the scandalmongers still were going at it in the newspapers and by word of mouth.

In a department store she overheard from strangers the worst of the slanderous charges that had hitherto been kept from her by her solicitous husband. She heard the charges; she heard her name; she knew now what the whole nation was talking about. And she was ashamed.

At home, Jackson became worried when she did not return from town. He sent friends looking for her everywhere. A group of them found her crouching in a corner of the store where she had overheard the gossip about her. She was terror-stricken and hysterical.

They took her back to the house as gently as they could. But Rachel Jackson was a very sick woman. It seemed that she had suffered a heart attack in the store after she had assimilated the news she had heard.

She was not a young woman; at sixty the complications that followed her apparent heart attack were too much for her. The emotional condition rendered by the tales she had heard had a deleterious effect on her physical condition. Several days later she died.

Andrew Jackson was beside himself with grief.

"In the presence of this dear saint, I can and do forgive all my enemies. But those vile wretches who slandered her must look to God for mercy."

Without Rachel, Andrew Jackson was a lonely, sad, and embittered man. She would have made the White House a better place to live than it was during Jackson's two terms. She was the First Lady who wasn't—and should have been. And her absence was due to vilifiers and scandalmongers who couldn't keep their clacking tongues silent.

8

The Degeneration Gap

Presidential sons have long felt the heat of public opprobrium. Franklin Delano Roosevelt had four sons and one daughter—and almost every one of them got into some hot water. But it was usually James, the oldest, who attracted the worst press.

Even in law school, after graduation from Harvard, he managed to give his father, who was then governor of New York, a few gray hairs. While in Boston, an insurance broker inveigled Jimmy into joining the firm. He was offered fifty dollars a week for less than forty hours of work.

Eleanor Roosevelt was ecstatic. "James has got a job!" she cried.

But FDR was "fit to be tied," as Jimmy described him. It smacked of nepotism to him, or influence peddling, or both—in other words, of everything reprehensible from a political standpoint.

In a fiery note he shot off to Jimmy in Boston, FDR cautioned him against allowing his name to be used for business favors, and said that sometime in the future he would explain "some of the reasons for the great willingness of some people to be awfully nice to you."

By 1933 FDR was in the White House, and the Boston press became vindictively loud in its denunciation of Jimmy. "James Roosevelt has virtually stepped into the role of patronage dictator, personally selecting officials for federal posts."

A big flap went up when Alva Johnston published an attack on him in the *Saturday Evening Post.* In the article "Jimmy's Got It," he hinted that the president's son used his family connections to increase his income from $250,000 a year to $2 million a year! He said that it came through his hefty insurance sales and from wielding his influence with potential insurance clients.

Colliers, the *Saturday Evening Post*'s main competitor, printed a Walter Davenport story correcting the allegations and stating that Jimmy really made $21,714.31 in 1933 and finally $49,167.37 in 1941. But of course, the damage had already been done. Jimmy became a favorite target for critics, cartooned everywhere as either the "crown prince" or the "assistant president."

Years later Jimmy said of it, "Possibly I should have been sufficiently mature and considerate enough of Father's position to have withdrawn from the insurance business entirely. But I was young, ambitious, spoiled—in the sense of having been conditioned to require a good deal of spending money—so I went right ahead in pursuit of what seemed to me the easiest solution."

In fact, Jimmy was never too bright about money matters. Just after he had graduated from Harvard, he made the Grand Tour of Europe and arrived in Ireland on the last lap. He found the country filled with choice horseflesh and a delightful array of even choicer race touts.

One of these smooth-talking Irish con men sold Jimmy a

colt for four hundred and fifty dollars, which was all the money he had for his passage home. Jimmy cabled his father informing him that he had bought a prize piece of horseflesh, and would his father send five hundred to cover his way home?

Roosevelt cabled back:

SO HAPPY ABOUT THE HORSE. SUGGEST BOTH OF YOU SWIM HOME. FDR.

Jimmy was forced to beg the fare from his grandmother, Sara Delano Roosevelt, who spoiled all the Roosevelt children outrageously and indiscriminately. She sent the money and he came home, somewhat chastened.

But not much.

By the time FDR gained the White House in 1932, James had married Betsey Cushing, the daughter of a famed Boston surgeon, and had settled down in the Bay Area. His income magically escalated through the new prestige of his name; opportunities unimagined before his father's elevation to the presidency presented themselves.

One of those other opportunities came from Joseph P. Kennedy, a man who had given $40,000, no strings tied, to get Jimmy's father elected. Kennedy was interested in making some money on whiskey futures, should Prohibition be repealed, as Kennedy felt sure it would be with FDR in the White House.

Kennedy and his wife, Rose, made friends with Jimmy and Betsey Roosevelt; after all, they were all good Democrats. In 1933 Joe and Rose Kennedy accompanied the young Roosevelts on a cruise to London. Kennedy didn't just want Jimmy's friendship; he wanted help in getting as many liquor franchises as he could get from English firms. He intended to get them at the horse's mouth—that is, in London—and sew up as many brands as he could before the United States went wet.

Then he could have *all* the profits in English imports.

Jimmy went along with it. It seemed to him to be a very

friendly relationship, and harmless. Using Jimmy's presence to give the proper aura of prestige and glamour, Kennedy succeeded in becoming exclusive sales agent for Haig and Haig, John Dewar, and Gordon's Dry Gin—and that meant that with repeal, good Scotch and honest gin all over America would be coming to you strictly through the courtesy of honest Joe Kennedy!

"The British didn't select their agents haphazardly," said one liquor distributor in the United States. "They felt Jimmy Roosevelt was a good connection, so they gave their lines to Kennedy."

Joe Kennedy then organized his own company, Somerset Importers, to stockpile thousands of cases of imported liquor—legally sent into the country at the time as "medicinal" goods—all to be marketed to the thirsty once FDR went through the motions of having the Eighteenth Amendment repealed.

Joe Kennedy made a tidy profit on that business venture. Jimmy Roosevelt didn't do quite so well. He had gone along with the project because he thought Joe Kennedy would cut him in as a partner in the enterprise. When Jimmy finally came out with the suggestion that he thought he should have a piece of the action, the patriarch of the Kennedy clan laughed him off. "Oh, you can't do that," he told Jimmy with a wave of his hand. "It would embarrass your father."

In April 1936, Louis Howe died. Howe was the president's right-hand man, a confidante closer than even the First Lady. He was missed by the president; FDR needed someone to step into his shoes.

Jimmy's bad press had been continuing in Boston. So the president decided that he could save Jimmy from his enemies and get himself a first-rate aide by appointing him to the White House staff.

The First Lady disagreed with the president's move. She warned him it would bring down on him a volley of political gunfire.

"Why should I be deprived of my eldest son's help and of the pleasure of having him with me just because I am the president?" FDR said.

FDR's first step was to commission Jimmy Roosevelt a lieutenant colonel in the Marine Corps at the age of twenty-nine. That would give him the proper rank to act as a military aide to the president during an extended tour of South America he planned to make.

There were screams of nepotism from every quarter, but FDR and Jimmy weathered the storm, and Jimmy proved to be a resourceful and much-needed personal crutch for the president. It was not long after the South American tour that FDR appointed him permanently to a job in the White House.

As aide Jimmy spent most of his time with his father, acting as his physical support. It was Jimmy on whom FDR leaned when he was out of his wheelchair seeing visitors or speaking in public. The American public did not know—and never knew during FDR's lifetime—the full extent of the president's disability.

Jimmy's job soon gave him ulcers. He was sent up to the Mayo Clinic for treatment. Tests showed no cancerous growths, but something had to be done about Jimmy's ulcer-wrecked stomach lining. Doctors decided to remove two-thirds of it.

The president visited the clinic at the time of the operation; it was that serious. The press hung around like hopeful vultures. The patient was out of the clinic in ten days, with only one-third of a stomach left.

Now strange reports began leaking out. Jimmy was in love. But not with his wife. He was carrying on, the inside stories went, with a nurse at the clinic.

In Washington Roosevelt was livid. Betsey was his favorite daughter-in-law. He dispatched Harry Hopkins to bird-dog the situation. But Romelle Schneider—she was the nurse—had already made her play. Jimmy decided to divorce Betsey to marry her.

The story made all the headlines. The publicity and notoriety centered on the White House family couldn't be worse for FDR's administration.

A confrontation was obviously in the making. The president was vindictive. Jimmy pleaded health considerations. He blamed his ulcers on his marital problems with Betsey. FDR was unamused.

The next step was obvious. Jimmy offered his resignation from the job, publicly pleading bad health. It was simply a gesture. With an alacrity that was ego-shattering to Jimmy, FDR accepted.

Then the president telephoned Basil O'Connor, one of the sharpest attorneys in New York and FDR's law partner, retaining him to represent Betsey in the forthcoming divorce action.

Jimmy fled to the West Coast. He managed to wangle a very good job as Samuel Goldwyn's assistant in the motion picture business, at a salary of $25,000 a year.

Shortly after that he did indeed divorce Betsey and marry Romelle Schneider. The president's wrath was great; but suddenly it all calmed down. Bigger things were on the horizon.

With Pearl Harbor, the United States was at war. Jimmy was already a Marine Corps officer, although his original commission as lieutenant colonel was reduced to captain. With only one-third of a stomach left he was ineligible for combat service, but he still managed to get on active duty. Soon he was appointed military adviser to William ("Wild Bill") Donovan, then the executive officer of Carlson's Raiders.

In 1942 Jimmy was in the Second Marine Raider Battalion, working in the Far East, promoted to major in 1942 and to lieutenant colonel in 1943. He was involved in combat in the South Pacific in Guadalcanal, Tarawa, Midway, and was then made full colonel.

A national magazine took pot shots at him during the war years. He was once referred to as a "hopelessly 4-F" reserve officer with gastric ulcers. However, the gist of the story went that he was using "his father's prestige shamelessly to get into the shooting."

On Makin Island, Jimmy was second in command to Lieutenant Colonel Evans Carlson in a bloody raid. The action was so close to the enemy that one of them shot a walkie-talkie out of Jimmy's hand as he scuttled across the beach. His heroism during the war years earned him the Navy Cross—the medal second only to the Congressional Medal of Honor—and the Silver Star.

After the war was over Jimmy settled in California, where he ran successfully for Congress. Later he went up against Earl Warren for governor, and lost.

When his marriage to Romelle Schneider went down the drain, he married Gladys Irene Owens in 1956. That marriage didn't last long, either, and in 1969 he married Mary Lena Winskill. Later he served with the United States delegation in the United Nations.

FDR once said about his own family: "One of the worst things in the world is being the child of a president! It's a terrible life they lead!"

Jimmy Roosevelt ought to know.

If Robert Johnson, the third of President Andrew Johnson's children, grew up to disgrace his father by his alcoholism and his inability to function properly, quite a bit of the blame should rest with his health problems and what he went through during the Civil War years, before he wound up in Washington to work for his father.

Born in 1834, Robert was the second of Andy Johnson's boys. He was a high-spirited, active, and daring young man. He went to school, then college, and read for the law. That, in spite of the fact that he continued to have hemorrhages all through his youth that worried every doctor he went to see. His health worries contributed to his early addiction to alcohol; even before he was a mature adult, he was a heavy drinker.

Robert had good rapport with his father; so did all Johnson's children. "Tell it as it is or not at all," he said to them constantly. None of his children feared him; they took their problems to him and he listened to them as objectively as he could.

Andy Johnson himself had come up the hard way. Apprenticed to a tailor, he had no formal schooling. At the time "readers" were hired by tailors to read books aloud to the apprentices and workers as they sat sewing. Johnson memorized the words he heard, managed to figure out how to read by putting the proper sound to the proper grouping of letters—and eventually became a tailor.

After his marriage to Eliza McArdle in 1827, Johnson set up a shop in Greeneville, North Carolina, and began what proved to be a thriving business.

People liked him and eventually elected him to the village council. Soon he was serving as alderman, and then mayor. By 1835 he was a member of the state legislature, then the state senate, and in 1853, he became governor of Tennessee.

The governorship was only a step up; in 1857, Johnson was elected to the United States Senate. He was in the Senate when the Southern States, including Tennessee, seceded from the Union in 1861.

Tennessee was a pivotal state, split between factions favoring the North and the South. Johnson opted to remain with the Union. Immediately he was declared a traitor at home, and the members of his family were forced to go underground.

In the summer and fall of 1861, Johnson remained in the capital, completely in the dark as to what had happened to any of his family. Finally, in October, he got a letter from a friend mentioning that Robert had said to tell Johnson that the family was all well. The letter took two weeks to reach the capital.

Meanwhile, Robert was trying to save his life and the lives of his immediate family. He and his older brother Charles, along with his sister Mary's husband, Daniel Stover, fled into the hills. There they gathered with other Union sympathizers and formed a resistance group to act as guerrillas against the Confederate soldiers in the area.

All of Andrew Johnson's property in Tennessee was confiscated by the Confederates, as was the land of other Northern sympathizers.

In January 1862, another letter was sneaked through the lines to Johnson. Charles, he learned, had "come out of the bush and taken the oath [to fight for the Union]." Robert was still "in the bushes." Mary's husband Stover might be on the way to Kentucky. A friend, Judge Patterson, had been arrested and freed by the Rebels. "Your house is now a Rebel *hospital* and the Rebels are cutting up Greeneville [a euphemism for 'dividing up the spoils']."

As the hue and cry against them diminished, the Johnsons came out of the "bushes." Many of them decided to volunteer for the Union army, thus becoming "Tennessee Vols." Robert was such a one. In the early months of 1862 he made a daring escape through the lines to a Union camp in Kentucky. It took him nine days to make the hazardous trip.

"If they had arrested me," he wrote his father in Washington, "I have no doubt that they would have hung me. I am almost broke down, but will leave here in a day or two, and hope to meet you in Washington in good health."

And he added: "It is impossible to put on paper, the scenes that have taken place in East Tennessee since you left."

Within two weeks, Robert was in Washington. There he was commissioned by Secretary of War Edwin M. Stanton as a colonel, to raise a regiment of volunteers in Tennessee. With the state mostly in Confederate hands at the time, it was a risky undertaking.

Robert went back into the hills and began gathering together the groups of guerrillas into the semblance of a regiment. In spite of the hazards, the group finally broke out of the Confederate-held territory, and became a legitimate Union unit.

The regiment, still in the formation stage, was sent to Ohio. It was there that the vaunted machinery of the military completely collapsed. The volunteers were months in the hills without any money or uniforms, living from hand to mouth, and trying to keep from starving to death.

The regiment had been ordered to Camp Spears, an isolated Northern outpost in Ohio where supplies were supposed to be waiting for them. It had taken the men eighteen days of hard marching from the Cumberland Gap on the Tennessee-Kentucky border to get to the camp. But at Spears there was nothing. They had no tents, no pay, no uniforms. All they owned were their own hunting rifles.

A dispatch from the War Department to Robert Johnson contained a brief message of congratulations on his success in raising the regiment of Tennessee Volunteers. Robert fired off the following response right back in the teeth of the generals in the War Department:

"My men are exiles from home—and never received any pay. My official instructions have been intercepted from the Secretary of War changing my regiment from Infantry to Cavalry. I have been in the mountains for three months. My men are naked, hatless, and shoeless. In the name of Heaven can you not relieve them? Answer me at this or whatever point our Brigade may be ordered."

A wire came from his father, in the Senate.

DO YOUR DUTY, the telegram read, AND ALL WILL COME OUT ALL RIGHT.

After clothing and equipment had been delivered, and his men outfitted, Robert was ordered back to Tennessee. He and his men pushed back into the war zone.

In the meantime, western and central Tennessee had fallen into Union hands. In 1862 President Lincoln appointed Robert's father, Senator Andrew Johnson, as military governor of Tennessee.

Johnson arrived in Nashville to handle administration of the Union half of the state. Confederate authorities decided then to expel the members of Johnson's family who were still in Greeneville as enemy agents. Johnson helped arrange a "prisoner of war exchange" to get them out.

Once they arrived in Nashville, the Johnson family was reunited for the first time since the war had begun. Johnson, never an emotional or sentimental man, broke down and wept when he finally set eyes on his family.

Robert's regiment became an official part of the Union army and moved back to Tennessee. His military training was not traditional, but derived from absolute necessity. Guerrillas did not fight like soldiers in the ranks. Robert was a successful guerrilla because he had an independent and self-reliant nature to begin with; many called him rebellious as well.

When his unit was amalgamated into the regular army, Robert seemed unable to adopt the disciplinary attitude of the typical commissioned officer—who gave orders, but who must also obey them without demur. He told off his superiors with a regularity that was disconcerting to them and vanished into the hills whenever he felt put upon, which was often. In direct defiance to orders, he drank heavily. He loved to hell around with his friends, of the lower ranks. He simply could not conform to military discipline. News of his scrapes with authority upset his father in Washington.

"Do your duty and all will come out all right," Johnson advised him again. He also cautioned him from association with certain "dangerous companions" whom he named.

But in Tennessee Robert only made himself more objectionable to his superiors and continued to get himself into trouble. On the eve of the Battle of Chattanooga—at the strategic moment when all the Union hopes hung in the balance and his father, as governor of Tennessee, was in a state of terrible suspense—Robert made his next spiteful move: He resigned his commission, claiming to his astonished superiors that his father had required it of him. This was too much for the governor. He wrote one of the few letters he ever posted to any member of his family.

"My dear son," he wrote. "Your note of the 17th is now before me. My [measure] of grief and love [has] been enough without your adding to them at this time. I have been determined that no act of mine should be an excuse for your recent course of conduct and do not now [mean] to depart from it. You tender your resignation predicted upon my wish for you to do so, and as I obtained the commission for you [I] have the right to require you to resign and therefore you do resign.

"I have not indicated to you by word or deed any desire on my part that you should resign your commission as Col. [sic] of the regiment; but on the contrary have expressed myself in the most emphatic terms that I would rather see you once more yourself again at the head of your regiment going to your own native home than be possessed of the highest honor that could be conferred upon me. In this so far I have been doomed to deep disappointment. I have said and now repeat that I feared you would be dismissed from the Army unless you reformed and took command of your regiment, and gave some evidence of a determination to serve the country as a sober, upright, and honorable man.

"I have also said further, that your own reputation and that of an exiled family required one of two things, reformation in your habits and attention to business, or to withdraw from the Army. One or the other is due yourself, the regiment, and the Government. . . . This is what I have said. It is what I now feel and think. Though [you are] my son, I feel I am not discharging the duty of a father who has devoted his whole life to the elevation of those he expected to leave behind him.

"In your letter you say my will is the law with you in reference to the resignation. I do most sincerely wish that my will was the law in regard to your future course. I would be willing this night [to] resign my existence into the hands of Him who gave it. Your devoted father. . . ."

Robert received the letter on the day the Battle of Chattanooga opened and immediately replied with an apologetic note. Robert swore that he would try to reform and become once again "a sober man."

However, he was now debating whether or not he should

make his resignation stick or whether he should get back in uniform. He needed his father's advice—and he got it.

The governor was called to Washington, and there Robert visited with him. "Taking everything into consideration, after mature reflection, I believe I will resign and try my future in some of the new territories," he wrote his father later. "Next Sunday is my birthday, and I have, in anticipation thereof, cast away forever my past conduct. . . . I *will* succeed . . . *the intoxicating bowl goes to my lips no more.*"

A florid style, a pale promise. In the end Robert did not actually quit the army, but joined his father's staff in Nashville, as his special aide. He remained there with him through the ensuing months of the war. Near the war's end Johnson was nominated as Abraham Lincoln's vice-president.

With Lincoln's assassination just days after the signing of peace, Robert and the rest of the family moved into the White House with the new president.

Now thirty-one, Robert became the president's personal secretary. Johnson obviously appointed him to the post so he could keep his eye on him.

In spite of his promises, Robert had not yet managed to stop his incessant drinking. In fact, he would still vanish for days on end without trace. And he would always return swearing off liquor—a promise he continually failed to keep.

By now Robert was a familiar figure in Washington. Everyone knew about the president's drunken son. The press was very down on him. Nor was his father's presidency suffering any less. He was surrounded by enemies who soon attempted to impeach him.

With Robert's appearances in many public places in a state of total inebriation, the president became desperate. He asked his secretary of the navy, Gideon Welles, to search for a place for Robert aboard some navy ship "bound on a distant cruise." Secretary of State William Seward was also asked for help. Seward liked Robert. He finally arranged to give him semiofficial diplomatic status and get him out of town. He was scheduled to ship out to Liberia, in Africa, to study the slave trade for a report to State.

Weeks of preparation went into the endeavor. When the captain of the ship finally called on the president to pick up Robert, he was nowhere to be found. As usual, he was out painting the town, an embarrassed sister admitted; what town, or part of it, she did not know.

Eventually, some months later, Robert did carry out the mission to the west coast of Africa. The mission cruise in no way stopped his drinking, however. After his return to Washington he continued to go on spree after spree, throughout his father's term of office.

When Johnson's term ended, Robert and the rest of the family followed him back home to Tennessee. But just a month after his father left the presidency, Robert became ill and died quite unexpectedly.

The Adamses were a family of overachievers in a time when it was normal for all Americans to try harder. But an Adams overachieved to a greater degree than any other overachiever. To be superlative in the Adams family was the accepted norm. To be mediocre in the Adams family was not tolerated. To be a loser was simply unheard of.

Most Adamses were superstars. Those who were not soon changed their ways and became superstars; then they were accepted. Those who could not were simply destroyed.

John Adams, the patriarch, was the star of the first generation. John Quincy Adams, the star of the second. It was the third generation in which George Washington Adams appeared. The oldest offspring, George had been born in Berlin while his father was United States minister there. His brother John was two years younger than he, and Charles Francis, six years younger.

George was the first Adams of his generation to graduate from Harvard, and soon after that he intended to set up a law practice in Boston. By now his father, John Quincy Adams, was secretary of state, on his way to the presidency. After graduation George visited his family in Washington to stay awhile before going back to the Bay Area.

Living in the Adams home at that time were two young nieces, Mary Catherine Hellen, the orphaned daughter of Louisa Adams's sister, and Abigail Adams, the daughter of George's uncle, Thomas Boylston Adams.

It was Mary Hellen who attracted the boys; at one time or another, all three of the Adams sons were in love with her. But it was George who took the giant step and became engaged to her on January 8, 1824. That was the occasion of a huge party at the Adams house celebrating the ninth anniversary of the Battle of New Orleans, a key victory in the War of 1812.

The second brother, John Adams II, was not quite as lucky as his older brother at Harvard. He, along with his entire senior class, was expelled for "rioting and insubordination." He was the first Adams not to graduate from the institution. It was an unfortunate business, but John was not really totally disgraced. The riot occurred over bad food and living conditions; expulsion was simply a face-saving device of the administration of the college. John moved to Washington to be with the family.

George went to Boston to get his law practice going. In 1825 John Quincy Adams, George's father, was elected the sixth president of the United States. He appointed his son John as his personal secretary. When Charles graduated from Harvard shortly after the inauguration, he too moved in with the family in Washington, spending about two years there—1824 to 1826—before returning to Boston and a job as clerk in Daniel Webster's law office.

While in Washington, Charles wrote a letter to George obliquely referring to George's romance with Mary Hellen. Charles warned George that the romance seemed doomed if George didn't do something about it—and do it quickly. He specified no details. Nor did he mention their brother John.

The president, who didn't want George to get married

quite so soon anyway, paid little attention to what was going on under his nose. George acted in somewhat the same manner as his father did, for his own reason. Whatever his motivation, he failed to heed his brother Charles's warnings, and did nothing. After two years, Charles left Washington for Boston, and it was then that the bombshell exploded.

In a letter to George from his mother, Abigail wrote that George's brother John Adams II and Mary Hellen were going to be married. She also said that neither she nor the president would have a thing to do with it. Eventually they did recognize it, but they did not enthusiastically endorse it.

When George heard that he had been jilted, he refused to communicate with either his lost fiancée or with his brother. Charles was annoyed at George. He thought his older brother should have accepted the situation without being so piqued. George's reaction betrayed to him, "more littleness of spirit than I had wished to suspect in him."

The marriage between John Adams II and Mary Hellen took place in February 1828; neither of John's brothers attended. Bitter animosity prevailed between both Charles and George and their brother John. Charles felt that John had acted badly toward George. The First Lady was totally apathetic about the wedding. She was "unwell" through most of the wedding festivities. The bride and nervous groom honeymooned at home in the White House.

However, Abigail did loosen up enough to write that "the bride looked very handsome in white satin, orange blossoms, and pearls." The wedding took place in the Blue Parlor, "arranged with flowers and ribbons." On the day following the ceremonies a White House reception was held for the newlyweds.

The president himself acted quite unlike an Adams. He danced at the wedding ball, a Virginia reel "with great spirit," as one observer said. The wedding, according to reports, was "a high-spirited affair with many guests and much laughter."

Adams sent a piece of the wedding cake to his son Charles,

writing that he hoped that the brothers—George and Charles—would bless the marriage.

They did not. George refused to talk to his younger brother, or even to write to him. The affair seemed to affect him more deeply than anyone would have expected. After all, an Adams was a man of the intellect and not of the heart.

But George eventually began to buckle, apparently under the pressure of the Adams ethic. He had become a member of the bar and had also been elected to the Massachusetts State Legislature, but he was found to be careless with his work and with his financial obligations.

He began to drink heavily. Was it because he lost his fiancée, now his sister-in-law? Was it something else? Was he fighting the self-discipline his father—any Adams—demanded of the clan?

In a dream, which turned out to be a kind of psychological nightmare, he saw again a young girl he had been interested in when he was a freshman at Harvard. During the dream his own father entered the scene to shake his finger at George admonishingly:

"Remember, George, who you are and what you are doing."

George awoke in a cold sweat, and wondered what it all meant.

Meanwhile, in Washington, his father had been defeated for reelection. He was planning to quit Washington forever, and wrote his son that he wanted help in packing his things for the move to Quincy. George's brother John was planning to stay with his wife and child in Washington.

Apparently George did not answer his father's letter. So Charles, who did not see him much, visited him at his father's request. He found his older brother quite sickly. George complained of dejection, low spirits, and melancholia. Charles knew that he had become a kind of recluse, keeping away from his old friends.

Charles had agreed to help his father and was ready to leave for Washington. He wrote a letter before he made the trip, explaining about George. He said his brother was "very much disarranged. He wants bracing and enlivening," he wrote to his mother. "His entire seclusion from society . . . and his want of occupation produce a listlessness peculiarly oppressive."

George did not want to go to Washington; there were too many bitter memories there for him. Besides, he knew if he went there he would have to see his brother John and his sister-in-law, Mary. But after a lot of indecision, George finally told Charles, just before he left, that he would make the trip by himself.

As it happened, George never did get to Washington. He started out, driving from Boston to Providence by carriage, and there took a steamboat, the *Benjamin Franklin*, bound for New York.

The next day, April 30, 1829, the following story appeared in the *New York American*:

"A very melancholy occurrence took place last night on board the Steamboat *Franklin*, on her passage from Providence to this city. George Washington Adams, eldest son of the late President [i.e., "past" president] of the United States, was on board on his way to Washington. During the day and evening he evinced no symptoms of indisposition till near bedtime, when he complained of a violent pain in his head, and said he would be bled as soon as he got to New York.

"He, however, retired with the other passengers but rose about 2 o'clock, dressed himself in a hurried manner and awoke one of the passengers, complaining they were plotting against him, and particularly asked one of them what it was he had said about his (Mr. Adams') jumping overboard. Nothing of the sort had been said, and the thing passed off, Mr. Adams going upon deck and the passengers resuming their slumbers.

"The only subsequent trace of the unfortunate young man was the finding some hours afterward of his hat upon the deck forward of the wheelguard whence he is supposed in a high state of fever to have jumped overboard. Mr. Adams was a lawyer of promise, a young man of considerable acquirements, and has been several times one of the representatives of the Massachusetts legislature of the city of Boston. He was unmarried."

The Adamses were prostrated by their son's suicide. Charles was greatly upset. "I wrote a few lines to my father, and I bent my soul in humble and fervent prayer that God would soften the stroke upon my poor afflicted parents." The former president assured Charles that he and his wife "still look for consolation in the affectionate kindness of our remaining sons."

But Charles felt guilt about his brother's death. He recalled that George had complained to his doctor, a physician named Walsh, before he left for Washington. Charles decided that he should never have permitted him to go alone. Filled with remorse, he went to George's room to look at his things.

It was there that the full picture of George's "other life" took shape before Charles's horrified eyes. Dr. Walsh had a chambermaid named Eliza Dolph. Sometime after Mary Hellen had abandoned him for his brother John, George had seduced Eliza. The girl had then given birth to George's illegitimate child.

But the situation was more complicated than that. Soon after Charles had learned the truth about his brother's bastard child, a building superintendent in Boston, named Miles Farmer, approached Charles with a blackmail attempt.

It was Farmer's story that in January a certain Dr. David Humphreys Storer had come to Farmer and proposed that he take into his family the illegitimate child, then about eight weeks old, "to restore the mother to her friends and society again."

George was continuing to see Eliza, Farmer said. Farmer's tenants were upset over the liaison, and were threatening his job. George had promised him $100 and protection if anyone asked probing questions. Now that George was dead, Farmer had neither the $100 nor George's protection. He demanded that Charles and the Adamses pay him off for his "discretion." After all, George was the son of a former president of the United States.

Charles wrote a letter to Farmer, refusing. Eliza, he told him, in typical Adams fashion, "must work for herself." The Adamses would pay no money to help. "She shall be in no worse situation than she was before this occurrence, so far as demands upon the money she may earn will go."

Farmer didn't get a cent. In a few months, Eliza returned to work as a domestic. "I will make some provision for the child probably similar to what it would be entitled [to] by law," Charles wrote Farmer.

This was not satisfactory to the would-be blackmailer. He threatened to make the sordid story public. But Charles stood fast. "You are welcome to all the benefit a disclosure will give you," he wrote Farmer.

Farmer turned to Dr. Storer, who had acted as go-between for George and Eliza. The squabble reached the Massachusetts courts. In 1831, three referees awarded Farmer $200 damages. Farmer was annoyed; he thought he should have got more. He issued a forty-four page pamphlet attacking both Storer and the Adamses.

Meanwhile Charles was as annoyed with Storer as he was with Farmer. When Storer submitted a bill against George's estate, Charles rejected it, since it did not specifically detail the number of times George had actually seen Eliza. Storer managed to collect $37 for his "services" to the chambermaid.

A suicide and a philanderer! And an Adams! It was a bitter pill for the stoic, intellectual, stern-lipped Adamses to have to swallow.

Stepsons cause as much worry as natural sons. James Madison, the fourth president of the United States, found that out when he married Dolley Payne Todd rather late in life.

Dolley had a son from her marriage to John Todd, a lawyer.

When Todd died of yellow fever, she was free to marry Madison, a rising figure in the capital.

They had no children of their own. Madison assumed the protection and guidance of Payne Todd, Dolley's beloved son. The term *beloved* was not used loosely either by Dolley or by Madison. She thought the world of the boy; possibly more than the world.

She often expressed herself about his welfare. During one of his sicknesses, she had written her sister:

"Payne continues weak and sick. My prospects rise and fall to sadness as this precious child recovers or declines."

She had frequently enjoined Madison to do everything he could for the child. Once in Philadelphia for an operation, she wrote her husband: "To find you love me, have my child safe and my mother well seems to comprise all my happiness. . . . Kiss my child for me."

And Madison did so. Both he and Dolley spared nothing to make the boy happy. As a result, he was probably one of the most spoiled youngsters in history. And he never really changed, even when he matured.

He went to all the best schools. When Madison realized the careless and indifferent boy needed closer supervision than he could get at home, he enrolled him in St. Mary's Academy in Baltimore, a Catholic school for boys open to non-Catholics. The school concentrated on foreign languages; it was strict on discipline.

Madison became president in 1809, and Payne Todd, as a graduate of St. Mary's, was about to be enrolled at the College of New Jersey—Princeton—where Madison himself had gone. But it never came about. In Washington Todd rode horseback, bet on the horses, danced with the girls, and thoroughly enjoyed all the perks of being the President's stepson. Why lose all that for four years of college?

Madison's secretary suddenly became ill and the president, despairing of Todd's ever leaving for college, put him to work in the job. In 1813 he sent Todd on a government mission to

St. Petersburg, Russia, where the Czar Alexander was mediating a settlement of the War of 1812.

Todd, then twenty-one, was appointed secretary to Albert Gallatin, one of the principal negotiators, and was made an honorary colonel in keeping with the prestigious assignment.

With Gallatin, Madison sent a draft for $800 for Todd, and he gave his stepson $200 on his own. He also told Gallatin that if Todd needed more, to "draw on him," that is, lend him the money for repayment later by the president. A thousand dollars in those days was a considerable sum.

When the group arrived in St. Petersburg, John Quincy Adams was serving as the American minister. He thought that Todd's importance was overblown. The young man seemed quite smitten with his own importance and tended to parade around ostentatiously in his colonel's uniform.

Todd aroused the interest of the Russian ladies. He was considered to be almost royalty in their eyes. He attended balls from which other members of the delegation were excluded, Adams reported testily.

After much backing and filling, the peace mission collapsed when the British declared themselves unwilling to negotiate with Gallatin. Madison decided to replace Gallatin with Henry Clay. Gallatin was called home.

Todd, however, left the official party with another aide to sail from St. Petersburg, by way of Göteborg, Sweden, and the Baltic Sea. He was icebound for weeks. Then, when it came time to leave Copenhagen, where he had eventually landed, he managed to miss the boat.

Gallatin's wife wrote to Dolley that Todd was not with the official party. Dolley was frantic. He had been gone fourteen months. The two were very close—or *had* been.

"I am distressed at Payne's leaving Mr. Gallatin. What could have led him to do so? Nothing but anxiety to get home I hope."

Not so. Todd had become involved in an incident in Russia

that almost blew up into an international crisis. The young colonel had swept a certain Countess Olga, otherwise unidentified, off her feet. They had become engaged to be married. Then the countess was suddenly and mysteriously abducted. She was not to be heard of ever again. Her aristocratic father had decided that no daughter of his would ever marry an untitled American.

Unable to locate his countess, and unable to interest any of his colleagues in helping him find her, Todd took to the vodka bottle. When the peace commission was recalled, he persuaded one of the other young aides, a man known only as Milligan, to leave the party and sail with him by way of the Baltic Sea.

Todd and Milligan finally caught up with the Gallatin group in Holland. But he rejoined them only for financial reasons. He was broke. Gallatin lent him money. He ordered Todd home, and Todd agreed to go—but by way of Paris. It would be a great cultural opportunity, of course.

"My precious Payne," Dolley wrote, "is going to France, and I hope to see him highly benefitted."

Soon the original three weeks in Paris had been extended to three months. And then Todd managed to miss another boat.

Madison's new peace mission began in Ghent, and the president told Todd to attend it. He did so. Gallatin, no longer in charge, was hearing bad reports from the American delegation about Todd: that he was so dissipated that he was helping no one—least of all himself, that he was indulging in heavy drinking bouts and all-night card games. Gallatin put on the pressure, but Todd said he was staying in Paris to be presented to Louis XVIII.

At home the war with the British continued. Washington was burned in 1814. On October 9, from Ghent, Todd wrote the president in part:

"My absence from Washington I most deeply regret if for no other reason [than that] I might at least have been useful to you and my mother [during the fire]."

The final peace treaty was signed on Christmas Eve in 1814. But Todd still did not come home. He had sent his luggage ahead, and it arrived in Philadelphia without him. Todd not only missed the boat at Le Havre, France, but again at Plymouth, England.

It was, in fact, after the battle of Waterloo, in 1815, that Todd finally returned to the United States. He had managed to borrow £1280 sterling—about $6,500 at the going rate of exchange—from the Baring Brothers of London.

"He has spent a longer time in Europe and more money than I wished," Gallatin wrote the president. His letter about Todd pointedly omitted any reference to the young man's value as a secretary to the commission.

Madison protested to Gallatin, but paid the money anyway.

Todd was restless in Washington. He found it was not as stimulating or exciting as Europe. During the racing season in October he was scheduled to meet some school friends at the Georgetown races, but as usual missed the event.

A friend wrote Gallatin: "Our friend Todd was *semper* Todd, and came to the race after it was over."

When Madison completed his second term in office, Todd opted not to follow his parents to Montpelier, their estate in Virginia. He was the complete urban sophisticate now. One friend said that he had finally "blossomed into the full maturity of his extraordinary power to distress his family."

Todd played on his stepfather's name wherever he went. He was always in the company of affluent friends, usually visiting the races and gaming tables and dropping bundles of money.

Dolley was unhappy. She wrote him: "But, my dear son, it seems to be the wonder of [all my friends] that you should stay so long from us, and now I am ashamed to tell, when asked, how long my only child has been absent from the home of his mother!

"Your papa thinks as I do that it would be best for your reputation and happiness, as well as ours, that you should have the appearance of consulting your parents on subjects of deepest account to you, and that you should find it so on returning to Philadelphia."

Upon receiving that epistle Todd's reaction was to borrow $400 from home. Later on he wrote, this time from Philadelphia, asking for money to pay coach fare home. It was forwarded to him. He did not appear, nor did he write.

A lottery house in Washington began dunning Madison for $500. He paid the money this time to keep Todd out of debtors' prison. But Madison was finally at the end of his patience. He wrote Todd that he was ashamed of his son and appalled at his ability to torment his mother. If Todd were to go to prison, "it would inflict new and untold tortures on her. Come then, I intreat and conjure you, to the bosom of your parents who are anxious to save you from tendencies and past errors and provide for your comfort and happiness."

Todd once again ignored the entreaty from home. By now Todd was involved in scandalous sexual concourse with loose women and in other problems. But Dolley luckily never knew the details, nor did Madison.

He avoided prison by borrowing $300 from the postmaster of Philadelphia, extracted because he was a friend of Madison's. Todd fled Philadelphia for New York. Now he was beginning to buy his liquor on credit.

More demands for payment came to Montpelier from Todd's creditors. Madison was forced to mortgage several of his farms to raise $5,600 to pay the bills. The usual crop failures plus a depression had made money exceedingly hard to come by.

Suddenly an enormous bill of $3,000 surfaced. Madison sold his entire tobacco crop, took another mortgage, and secured another loan. With this money, he staved off the inevitable a bit longer. But in June 1829, Todd finally was unable to charm his way out of the hands of the sheriff and went to debtors' prison.

Dolley was beside herself with grief. She wrote to Todd, pointing to the poor state of his father's health and what his antics were doing to it. Madison finally borrowed $400 from James Madison Cutts, his nephew, and sent it to free Todd from prison.

Todd never came home. The following year he was in jail again, his creditors dunning him for $600 in cash and promissory notes. This time when the debt was paid, Todd showed up at Montpelier, thin and ailing. He said he was totally through with spending money and drinking, and was eager to use his time in the country to rehabilitate himself. He had turned over a new leaf, he said.

Madison put him to work copying out his public papers. In the files was a sheaf of notes showing that Madison had paid out about $20,000 on Todd's debts without his wife's knowledge.

When Madison died, Dolley moved away from Montpelier to Washington where her nieces took care of her. Todd was left with the operation of the estate. Within a few years it was put up for sale. When the money from the sale went, Todd sold the president's personal papers to Congress for $30,000. That money, too, quickly disappeared. Dolley, scrimping along on next to nothing, then pawned her extensive collection of silver, the pride of the White House, to help him live.

Congress later bought the balance of Madison's unpublished papers from Dolley for $25,000. This time the money was put in a trust fund, to be received by Todd in installments. By now everyone recognized his total depravity.

Dolley Madison was eighty-one when she died, leaving a home she had purchased near the White House to her son and to a niece who lived nearby.

Todd refused to share the house with the niece, and sued in court to nullify the will. When that didn't work, he tried another of his multifarious money-raising schemes. He hired a professional collector who was trying to get money from him and assigned him to the job of administering the estate.

The collector was able to winnow out several of Madison's

important personal papers and letters. Todd sold them to private collectors. Years later these papers surfaced in various collections. The Library of Congress eventually purchased most of them from the owners.

At sixty-one, still unmarried, Todd was helling about and enjoying life as usual. He caught typhoid fever in 1853 and died after a brief illness.

"I have been my own worst enemy," he said as he lay dying. "I have harmed only myself." It was a smug assessment, and an erroneous one. He apparently never realized that by his innumerable antics he had hurt deeply not only his stepfather but had wounded his own mother terribly and irrevocably.

Five children were born to John and Abigail Adams, the second president and First Lady of the United States: Abigail Amelia, called "Nabby"; John Quincy, who became the sixth United States president; Susanna, who died in infancy; Charles; and Thomas Boylston.

The Adamses were a closely knit family—but a family that fate forced apart from the very first. In 1778 John Adams was sent by Congress to Europe to bolster the French alliance and to try to secure economic aid. He took along his oldest son, John Quincy Adams, then ten. Two years later they returned home, but Adams was soon sent back to Paris, and this time he also took along Charles, the middle son. The two boys were sent to Latin School at Amsterdam, to prepare for admission to Leyden University in the Netherlands.

But Charles, then only nine, was not old enough to enroll; the minimum age for admission was twelve. Charles was sent home to America alone, under the care of a family friend, Major William Jackson. With Jackson, Charles sailed from the Texel in the Netherlands on board the frigate *South Carolina*, with Captain Alexander Gillon at the helm. That was in August 1781,

It soon developed that Captain Gillon was more an adventurer with an eye to the main chance than the safe proprietor of a passenger ship. He kept changing his ports of call every time he heard of new freight to take on or a trade to make. Quite soon he and some of his passengers were in open opposition. Jackson took him to task verbally over the many delays that were keeping the ship from progressing toward America.

Soon the food was gone and the ship was forced to put into port at La Coruña, Spain, to take on provisions and water. There had been an abnormal amount of weather damage to the ship; it needed repairs, too.

Jackson quarreled with Gillon and, along with some of the other passengers, bought passage on another ship. This was the privateer *Cicero*, under the command of a certain Captain Hill.

Hill's ship was no luckier than the *South Carolina*. The passage was beset by delays and weird adventures, even from La Coruña to Bilbao, some three hundred miles along the Bay of Biscay. There were extensive negotiations with a mutinous crew and other delays due to provisioning and loading of goods.

Then the ship lay for weeks in Porto, Portugal. A friend of the Adams family was astounded to run into Charles and Jackson wandering about the streets of the city.

Finally the *Cicero* arrived in America belatedly on January 21, 1782, some six months later, making port at Beverly, Massachusetts.

Adams heard plenty about that trip from his wife, Abigail. "Ah! how great has my anxiety been," she wrote him. "What have I not suffered since I heard my dear Charles was on Board and no intelligence to be procured of the vessel for 4 months after she sailed. Most people concluded that she was founderd at Sea, as she sailed before a violent Storm."

Adams tried to calm his wife, but she never let him forget the incident. To Charles it seemed rather a lark, although in some ways, the young boy never really recovered from that harrowing experience.

When Charles finished his early schooling he was enrolled

at Harvard, where he breezed through his studies with a minimum of attention to details and a maximum of attention to recreation. Charles had always been darkly handsome, with a quick, bright mind and a totally ingratiating manner. In fact, he had grown more darkly handsome than ever and was breaking feminine hearts all around the Harvard Yard.

Abigail began worrying, reminding her husband that temptation and terrible dangers lay in wait for the weak or careless. She had reason to worry. There were near relatives on both sides of the family who had fallen prey to liquor: A brother-in-law, Robert Cranch, was a drunkard and ne'er-do-well, without even a suit of clothes to put on his back. William Smith, Abigail's wastrel brother, was a heavy drinker accused of having counterfeited money; Smith had abandoned his wife and children to live with another woman; he was deep into alcohol and total dissipation. Charles Warren, another relative, had succumbed in Spain to a virulent disease that might have been venereal in origin. A brother was being sued for two thousand pounds for assault and battery.

Abigail wrote frantically to John Quincy: "I hope you will guard your brother against that pernicious vice of gaming too much practiced at the university!"

Even John Adams, now vice-president, added his note of warning. "Never fail to walk an hour or two every day," he wrote Charles. He felt it would help keep his mind off vice and intemperance.

Charles was quick-witted, fast-talking, and easy-going—a companion favored by both men and women. He could talk his way through any group of cronies and dance his way through any group of women he met.

And yet beneath the intellectual surface of wit and charm there was an unseen instability that seemed to be eating away at his psyche.

Just as Abigail had feared, he fell in with a fast crowd and became involved in a number of escapades that did not endear him to his father. There were heated exchanges between the two.

In spite of the boy's fast life, he graduated very high in his class and moved to New York soon afterward to open up a law practice. His father was now vice-president; in 1790 the capital was established in New York City. Where better to have Charles than right under the observant eyes of Abigail and John? But in 1791, the capital was moved to Philadelphia, leaving Charles on his own.

As for Charles, how could a law practice fail when his own father was the number-two man in the country?

While in New York starting his law practice, Charles boarded out at the home of his sister Abigail's in-laws, the Smiths. His sister Nabby had been married to Colonel William Stephens Smith in England a few years prior to Charles's graduation. The Smith home was the obvious place for Charles to go.

Living now in Philadelphia, Abigail visited Charles frequently and found him in excellent health and spirits. "Charles is well, fat, and handsome, and persists in the line of conduct which we so much approved. His business increases and he will do very well." So she wrote in 1793.

That was wishful thinking. Abigail failed to perceive what was *really* happening. Boarding with the Smiths, Charles had his eye on Sarah Smith, Nabby's sister-in-law. It wasn't long before Charles succumbed to her charms and asked her to marry him. She was in love with him and accepted his proposal.

The vice-president was beside himself with anger and frustration. What was wrong with Charles? Why couldn't he behave like his self-sacrificing brother John Quincy, who had renounced his first love because he had no money to care for her? It was obvious that Charles lacked any common sense. He was making no money to speak of; he could barely support himself, much less a wife. Sally (Sarah) Smith was used to the good things in life. How could they survive?

The relationship between the vice-president and his second son became strained and unhappy from that moment on, never to be right again. Adams absolutely forbade the marriage to occur. There were unhappy scenes between the two Adamses—the one mature and dignified, the other brilliant, cutting, and unstable.

The situation languished in a stalemate for several months. Adams was too busy to interfere unduly. Abigail tried to keep her hand in, but apparently the two parents trusted their son too much.

In spite of the displeasure and obvious hurt of his parents, Charles and Sally were married in August 1795. He was twenty-five, handsome but totally insolvent. The two of them settled down in New York and hoped for the best. But it did not come.

Soon Charles and Sally had a child. Abigail visited them in New York, where they were living "prettily but frugally," as she told her husband in 1797. "He has . . . a discreet woman, I think, for his wife, quite different from many of the family." Abigail was referring to the general run of her luxury-loving and improvident relatives.

Nevertheless, Abigail sensed a kind of dissolution in her son. The next time she visited him, he was suffering from dysentery.

"To Charles I gave a puke last night and his complaints have abated," she told her husband. Charles, she thought, was drinking too much, and was not attending to his business. From Sally, Abigail learned that he was sinking into long periods of depression. Sally was beside herself with worry, and did not know what to do about it.

John Adams was elected president in 1797, and took office in 1798. His work kept him close to Philadelphia. Meanwhile Charles had begun to look with contempt on the practice of law. There simply wasn't enough money in it for him to support himself and his family. Rather than admit that his father had been right—that he should have waited longer to take a wife—he began to dabble in quick-buck enterprises.

A most successful fly-by-nighter of the day was Dr. Thomas Welsh, a land speculator. Welsh had a silver tongue, and very good luck when he started his real estate manipulations. Some of Charles's friends put money into Welsh's land schemes, and all seemed to make money.

Charles didn't have much of his own, but John Quincy was doing very well for himself, and Charles persuaded his brother to put money into Welsh's speculations. He borrowed money himself and invested. It looked like a sure thing.

Then suddenly—almost overnight—Welsh was broke. John Quincy's money was gone. So was Charles's. Nabby's husband, Colonel Smith, lost eighteen thousand dollars. The Adamses seemed beset with bad luck.

The president visited his son in New York in 1798, with unhappy results. Charles was still stunned over the loss of his brother's money—money he had persuaded him to invest in Welsh's doomed schemes. Charles seemed to his father to have deteriorated both in manner and in appearance. He was absentminded and vague in speech. His emotional state was unsatisfactory.

Charles's wife Sally told the president that Charles was frequently away from the house and when he returned he would be roaring drunk. After his hangovers had left him, he usually sank into dispiritedness and physical sickness.

His law practice had almost completely disintegrated. Creditors were waiting outside his house to harass him. His speculations on real estate had done him in. Although he never said anything about it, it was obvious that he felt overwhelming guilt over causing the loss of his brother's money in the Welsh debacle.

Even the president could not cheer up his son, and he left New York with a heavy heart.

Less than a year later, Charles took off to vanish in the city's tenderloin district. Sally had to give up the house and take her two children to move in with Nabby and her husband. The president visited her and was appalled.

"I pitied her, I grieved, I mourned," he wrote Abigail. He

was beside himself with anger and resentment. "I renounce him," he wrote of Charles. "King David's Absalom had some ambition and some enterprise. Mine is a mere rake, buck, blood, and beast."

What had happened to his son? With a Harvard education, sound legal training, the best of prospects, he had steered himself only to destruction, while everyone who loved him watched, unable to help him.

Finally Charles crawled back home, almost completely done in by drink and dissipation. This time Abigail came to visit him. Charles was so pathetically happy to see his mother that the pain and humiliation turned him into a sobbing wreck in front of her. He even asked after his father's health. Then he gave his mother a rambling and almost incoherent story of the bad breaks and the fateful mistakes that had reduced him to his present state.

Abigail could hardly believe her ears and eyes. Once the most charming and handsome of her sons, Charles was now a broken man, sunken deep into misery and despair. Where were those days of endless dancing and witty stories, of singing and flute playing?

The election of 1800, between Jefferson and Adams, was a wild and woolly affair, with Adams representing the Federalists and Jefferson the then-called Republicans. Jefferson won. Adams had become the first one-term president.

It was at the time the disappointed Adams was gloomily counting the votes and finding himself short of enough to win that Abigail once again stopped in New York to visit their ailing son.

Charles was absolutely destitute and desperately ill. He had a racking, consumptive cough, a very dangerous liver infection, and dropsy. He was not even living with Sally anymore. Sally had gone to her mother with the children. A friend had taken Charles in; it was obvious to everyone that he did not have long to live. Sally came by every day to nurse him in his last hours.

When Abigail left, she said a tearful good-bye to him, knowing it was to be her last.

"His physician says he is past recovery," she wrote her sister. "I shall carry a melancholy report to the president, who, passing through New York [recently] without stopping knew not his situation."

On November 30, 1800, Abigail's worst fears were realized. Charles died of cirrhosis of the liver, leaving his wife Sally and two young daughters.

"His constitution was so shaken," Abigail wrote, "that his disease was rapid, and through the last period of his life dreadfully painful and distressing. . . . His mind at times was much deranged thro his sufferings."

At first the lame-duck president was inconsolable. He mourned the "melancholy death of a once beloved son." He went on: "I might have died for him if that would have relieved him from his faults as well as his disease."

He called him "a Son who was once the delight of my Eyes and a darling of my heart, cut off in the flower of his days, amidst very flattering Prospects by causes which have been the greatest Grief of my Life." He had quite forgotten his earlier diatribe against Charles when he had visited Sally and the children at Nabby's and first learned in detail the facts about his debaucheries.

Charles's death was a bitter blow to the proud Adams family. Nor was it ever forgotten that Charles had gone against the general righteous and upward direction of the Adamses. Two years before, Adams had written, thinking of Charles, a quite accurate summation of his relationship as a father: "My children give me more pain than all my enemies."

9

The Papas and the Mamas

"My dad was a typical Irishman," Jack Reagan's son once said. "Happy-go-lucky, jolly, very sensitive—too much on the juice."

John (Jack) Edward Reagan was a first-generation black Irishman who lapsed from Catholicism and married a Protestant from a Scots-English background. Nelle Wilson, as her son Ronald Wilson Reagan wrote of her later in his autobiography, *Where's The Rest of Me?*, "had the conviction that everyone loved her just because she loved them." Jack was a cynic; Nelle was an idealist. Jack was a hard worker, but a heavy drinker; Nelle was a do-gooder, always trying to help people.

Jack supported his family during times when it was not easy to come by a dollar by selling shoes in various small-town stores throughout Illinois.

"He was a man who might have made a brilliant career out

of selling," Ronald Reagan said of him in his autobiography, "but he lived in a time—and with a weakness—that made him a frustrated man."

His weakness was alcohol. Ronald remembered one memorable encounter with his father while Jack was "on the juice." He came home one evening when he was about eleven years old to find his father passed out cold and slumped down on the front porch. It was cold out and snowing, and Ronald knew he had to get him in out of the storm.

Jack was dead to the world, snoring there, with his arms outstretched, almost as if, Ronald noted, he were crucified. The boy stood there a long moment, wondering what to do. He was tempted to go into the house and pretend he hadn't seen his father. It wasn't quite that easy, however. Somewhere along the line he had accepted his father's weakness and had decided to treat it as an illness that should be nursed. And yet it was hard to admit that his father was weak and a victim of a temptation he could not resist.

Ronald wrote later that he felt a sorrow for his father as he stood there, and a self-pity that was hard to overcome. However, his better impulses took over and his resentment passed.

"That was Nelle's doing," Ronald wrote. "With all the tragedy that was hers because of his occasional bouts with the demon in the bottle, she told [my brother] Neil and myself over and over that alcoholism was a sickness—that we should love and help our father and never condemn him for something that was beyond his control."

He decided he would drag his father inside. He reached down and grabbed a handful of his overcoat. Even though Jack was a heavy man, Ronald managed to pull him in through the open door and got him into his bed. And, of course, when Jack recovered within a few days, he was the same wise-cracking, smiling person he had always been.

In spite of his sales ability and cheerful exterior, Jack Reagan never made it. When Ronald succeeded in Hollywood some twenty years later, Jack and Nelle moved to the West

Coast and into a little cottage that Ronald had bought for them. It was the first piece of property that Jack Reagan ever owned. Ronald called it "the most satisfying gift of my life."

Jack was a natural storyteller, a raconteur par excellence, with an ebullient and puckish sense of humor that burst out in unexpected moments. He was particularly skilled at the kind of locker-room wit that was popular in those days before it became acceptable in night clubs and on television.

Ronald's skill with and interest in one-liners obviously was an inherited trait from his bouncy and down-to-earth salesman father. Luckily he did not inherit his father's weakness for alcohol.

From his mother Dwight David Eisenhower inherited quite a different kind of trait. She was a cheerful, optimistic woman with a sunny nature. Like her, her son became an optimistic, cheerful, and sunny man, even when he was in charge of the largest war machine in history.

But her son failed to inherit one of Ida Stover Eisenhower's most treasured beliefs; her faith in the Biblical commandment *Thou shalt not kill.*

When her son won an appointment to West Point, Ida and Dwight's younger brother Milton accompanied him down to the railroad depot in Abilene, Kansas, to bid him good-bye on his trip East. There was no sign of emotion in his mother as the train pulled out and he waved to her from the window. But as soon as she and Milton reached home, she ran upstairs and closed herself in her bedroom where she wept away the rest of the afternoon.

Ida Stover had grown up with relatives who were members of the Brethren in Christ, a Mennonite sect, deeply religious, moral, and severe. She had been educated at Lane University, a college run by the Brethren. It was not at all surprising that she was adamantly against war and adamantly for peace; many Americans were pacifists in those days.

Sometime after her son Dwight had become a career officer

in the army, and her other five sons had left home, she and her husband became bored with the conventional church services they attended in Abilene. The two of them joined with neighbors to hold weekly Bible study sessions at each other's homes.

Before long, most of them became involved with a sect called Jehovah's Witnesses. However, neither Ida nor her husband, David, chose to become aggressive evangelists in the manner typical of Jehovah's Witnesses. They stayed at home and refused to preach the message from door to door.

When David Eisenhower died in 1942, at the age of almost eighty, the trauma was too much for Ida, who was a year or so older than her husband. As a result of her shock she suffered an almost total loss of memory and severe mental disorientation. But she handled her fuzzy memory stoically and with a graceful humor.

The story goes that Milton Eisenhower, at the time president of Kansas State College, would drive over to the house for Sunday dinner and would chat with his mother after the meal was over.

"What did we have for dinner, mother?"

Ida would concentrate on that and then smile. "It was good, wasn't it?"

Or he might say, "Mother, I'll bet you can't name your sons in their proper order of birth."

And she would respond, "You know them as well as I do, Milton!"

Several of the Eisenhower sons finally arranged for a practical nurse to take care of her. Naturally, most of the people Ida knew were members of the Witnesses. And when the nurses began driving her through the small neighboring towns in Kansas to pass around leaflets from door to door, she did not object. She did not really know what was happening.

Perhaps she did not read the leaflets. The Witnesses did not believe in personal allegiance to anything but the second coming of Christ. Therefore, allegiance to the flag, or to a country, was not allowable in their orthodoxy. Saluting the flag and pledging Allegiance to the Flag were also forbidden.

The situation was a bizarre one at best. Here was Dwight D. Eisenhower, head of the invasion forces fighting to free Western Europe from the tyranny of Adolf Hitler; and here was Ida Eisenhower, his mother, distributing leaflets inciting her neighbors to refuse to salute the U.S. Flag.

Word soon got out to the Eisenhower sons, and a new companion was hired for their mother.

The story of Ida's leaflet distribution made the newspapers. Later on, during the administration of Dwight David Eisenhower, he received frequent letters noting the fact that he had a mother who was a Jehovah's Witness, and accusing him of never admitting the fact.

Ida Eisenhower died in 1946, at the age of eighty-four—some six years before her son became the thirty-fourth president of the United States.

Jesse Root Grant was a man who knew everything—at least, he thought he did. He also thought he knew how to do everything better than anyone else.

His son, Ulysses S. Grant, didn't inherit his father's opinionated view of himself, but he did inherit some of his stubbornness, a trait that stood him in good stead when he became the head of the Union army during the Civil War. Yet Jesse's strong-willed personality haunted his son all during his early service years, during his Civil War years, and during his White House years.

A tanner by trade, Jesse Grant was a penny-pinching, shrewd, calculating merchant, who didn't bother to communicate much with anyone else—unless he stood to make a profit.

He was all business. Only once during his more or less youthful years did he display a characteristic that was even halfway human. When a neighbor wrote a bit of doggerel verse to the newspaper, confiding that he needed a new pair of shoes, Jesse Grant came up with the following verse, which was printed in the same paper:

> Backwoodsman, sir, my aged friend,
> These lines in answer back I send,
> To thank you for your rhyming letter,
> Published in *The Castigator*.
> The story of your worn-out shoes,
> Is, to a tanner, no strange news. . . .
> And though I have not much to spare,
> I can, at least, supply a pair. . . .

It has to be mentioned that even though Jesse did show himself to be somewhat human in penning the verse, he did it strictly for a potential profit—selling shoes.

It was said that when Ulysses S. Grant told his father that he refused to become a tanner because the smell of curing leather sickened him, Jesse threw him out of the house. Young Grant then told his father he wanted to go to college. Jesse refused: It would cost money. He had the money, but he wasn't about to waste it on education for his son.

Still young Grant refused to take up tanning. It occurred to Jesse that he could get his son a proper college education—if that was what he wanted—by sending him to West Point. And Old Jesse wouldn't have to spend one red cent! The U.S. government would foot the bill.

Jesse then wrote to his congressman, proposing his son as a candidate. The congressman, Thomas L. Hamer, was a Democrat who knew Jesse Grant, a Republican, very well through his many fulminations against him both in the newspapers and among friends. When Jesse's missile arrived, Hamer realized that he might be able to cool Jesse's anti-Democratic fervor somewhat if he did him a favor and sent young Grant to West Point. And so he gave Grant the appointment.

Grant's career with the army was not an auspicious one. In 1853 he was in California, stationed at Fort Humboldt, about 250 miles from San Francisco, in the redwood country north of the Bay Area. He had left his wife and family back in St. Louis. It was a lonely, rugged outpost and the duty was filled with boredom. In addition, Grant's commanding officer was an old personal enemy from his Jefferson Barracks days, earlier in his career.

All this contributed to Grant taking to the bottle. He tried to get posted to a place nearer home so he could see his wife and children but there was no action on his request. He also came into collision with his commanding officer, who cited him for drinking on duty and accused him of other derelictions. Ironically, the army soon promoted him to captain. However, by then he had had it with the army, and on April 11, 1854 he wrote two letters: one a formal acceptance of his captaincy; the other a letter of resignation from the army.

The drinking, and the conflict with his commanding officer, and his loneliness all contributed to his decision. However, back home it appeared as if he had been cashiered out of the army for alcoholism.

His father was stunned. He even went so far as to write Jefferson Davis, then secretary of war, pleading with him to reinstate his son in the army: "I think after spending as many years in the servis [sic] he will be poorly qualified for the pursuits of private life," Jesse Grant wrote. "I will remark that he has not seen his family for over two years and has a son nearly two years old he has never seen. I suppose in his great anxiety to see his family he has been induced to quit the servis."

Jesse suggested a six-month leave of absence as an alternative. The War Department replied bluntly that Grant's resignation could not be reconsidered. The letter indicated that Grant "had assigned no reasons why he desired to quit the service and the motives which influenced him are not known to the Department."

It was an embarrassment to Grant when he discovered what his father had done. He accused him of meddling, but his father simply told him somebody had to fight for him.

Needless to say, that did not sit well with Grant, who was at the nadir of his life. Soon after that he went broke farming, then tried unsuccessfully to be a merchant, then a tanner, working for his brothers—but nothing came out right. He was saved by the Civil War, when after some complicated maneuverings on his own part and on the part of friends, he was given a commission once again and sent into action.

Jesse retired to live in Covington, Kentucky. Deciding he had an inside track with his son, he tried to get a contract to sell cavalry saddles to the army. After all, horsemen needed saddles; and Jesse was in leather.

His son had to turn him down. "I cannot take an active part in securing contracts," he told his father. "It is necessary both to my efficiency, to the public good and my own reputation that I should keep clear of Government contracts." Later he said, "I want always to be in a condition to do my duty without partiality, favor or affection."

Jesse was disappointed, but not discouraged. He decided to wait for another chance.

When Grant's military successes began, Jesse saw a chance to help his son fight his battles. It occurred as a result of a confrontation between Grant and General Henry W. Halleck over a personal misunderstanding, which boiled up into a nasty brawl, shortly after Grant's victory at Fort Donelson.

The trouble between Halleck and Grant was one of personality and perspective. Halleck was an intellectual who relied on battle analysis and strategic subtleties; he preferred studying war to fighting it. Called "Old Brains," he had no love for Grant's blunt, coarse, and practical methods.

After the battle in which Grant first took Fort Henry and then Fort Donelson, capturing 15,000 Rebels in the process, and issuing a note demanding "unconditional surrender," he found himself famous. It was the North's first real victory in the conflict.

Grant was accustomed to move about among his troops quite freely, and this annoyed Halleck, who wanted him close at hand. After a reprimand, which failed to change Grant's ways, Halleck complained to General George B. McClellan, his superior in charge of the Union army.

McClellan wrote back: "Do not hesitate to arrest [Grant] at once, if the good of the service requires it, and place General [C. F.] Smith in command."

The trouble blew over, but the news of the internal scrap leaked to the press. The press began needling Grant, with anti-Lincoln newspapers doing their best to rip him to shreds.

This didn't please the Old Man, Jesse Grant, sitting it out in Covington and reading the newspapers. He wrote a confidential letter to several of his son's aides asking for the truth about the matter. Letters came to him, defending his son and supporting his actions. Jesse shot one of these letters off to the newspapers; it was published.

Grant almost came home and wrung his father's neck in person. Instead he simply blew up by letter.

Jesse argued back. He felt his communication to the newspapers had "a salutary effect on public sentiment in this part of the country." Grant did not, and telegraphed Jesse not to publish anything more.

Jesse lay low for perhaps a year. But when the Battle of Shiloh came along, the newspapers began their attacks on Grant anew. Jesse couldn't stay out of it any longer. Shiloh was unquestionably a Union victory, in spite of the fact that Grant's activities were short of expectations.

"An investigation should be made of the utter inefficiency and incompetency, if not the downright treachery, of the generals," screamed the *New York Tribune* on April 16, after revealing that the Confederates had been defeated.

"Let us have the facts!" it editorialized. "Why does not General Grant tell the truth?"

Jesse Grant began to scribble letters to the newspapers, to friends, and to everyone who could read, defending his son's military strategies and downgrading the other generals.

It was all too much for Grant. He fired off this missile to his father in early 1862:

"I would write you many particulars, but you are so imprudent that I dare not trust you with them; and while on this subject let me say a word. I have not an enemy in the world who has done me so much injury as you in your efforts in my defense. I require no defenders and for my sake let me alone. I have heard this from various sources, and persons who have returned to this army and did not know that I had parents living near Cincinnati have said that they found the best feeling existing towards me in every place except there. You are constantly denouncing other general officers and the inference with people generally is that you get your impressions from me. Do nothing to correct what you have already done but for the future keep quiet on this subject."

Apparently his plea was effective, for his father simmered down for a while. But he was back in action during the siege of Richmond, when he came running down to visit his son. He had his usual get-rich-quick scheme: If he could get a corner on all the hides of cattle slaughtered for the army, he could make a fortune. He asked his son bluntly for the concession.

Grant shook his head. "No hides for you."

"But I don't want them for *nothing*. I'll make a bid for them like anybody else."

"If you can't see why you shouldn't bid for them, I don't believe I could enlighten you even if I should tell you."

Jesse went away with his dreams of a financial killing in leather unrealized.

He was somewhat muzzled for the rest of the war, although he occasionally fired off a fulmination to the press. But with his son's escalating popularity, and the war turning in the favor of the Union army, these diatribes were simply smiled at, and filed for later action.

Grant became solidly entrenched with the Lincoln administration before the end of the war, and was friendly with

President Andrew Johnson after Lincoln's assassination. He prevailed upon Johnson to give his father the postmastership at Covington, where Jesse lived. The post kept Jesse quiet for a while.

When Grant finally assumed the office of president after the election of 1868, Jesse began making quick trips to the capital. However, from the beginning, the First Lady's father, Colonel Frederick Dent, had installed himself in the White House, living there in imitation of a country squire. He read newspapers, drank mint juleps and smoked big cigars. He couldn't keep his mouth shut, any more than Jesse Grant could, discoursing continually on the "damned Yankees" and upstart "niggers." He amused some of the visitors, but not all of them.

One in particular who couldn't stand him was Jesse Grant. When he came to Washington on visits, he usually put up at a hotel down the road. "The White House," he told the press, "is full of the tribe of Dents. I simply don't like them."

Grant's mother, Hannah, was no problem. Although he asked her to the capital again and again, she never came. She gave no reason why she would not. Characteristically, she said as little as her husband said a lot.

On one occasion, when Grant came to visit her after he had become the head of the winning army in the Civil War, she came out to greet him, dressed in her old apron.

"Well, Ulysses, you've become a great man, haven't you?" That was all she said. Then she went on with her household tasks.

She was right, of course, but the way she said it, he could have been somebody else's son.

Abraham Lincoln's parents were not around when he occupied the White House. Both had died many years previously.

But Lincoln never failed to pay tribute to his mother—whom he considered a saint in spite of her less than saintly beginnings.

"All that I am or hope ever to be I get from my mother, God bless her," Lincoln said once about her. Then, in order to give the tribute the cutting edge it deserved, he continued:

"Did you never notice that bastards are generally smarter, shrewder and more intellectual than others? Is it because it is stolen?"

Lincoln's mother, Nancy Hanks, was an illegitimate child. For some five generations there had been Hankses in Virginia, near the area where George Washington, James Madison, James Monroe, and Robert E. Lee were born.

Nancy Hanks, by Lincoln's own estimation, was not of their social standing. In a paragraph he wrote about his forebears, he said:

"I was born February 12, 1809, in Hardin County, Kentucky. My parents were both born in Virginia, of undistinguished families—second families, perhaps I should say. My mother, who died in my tenth year, was of a family of the name of Hanks."

Nancy's grandfather, Joseph Hanks, had five sons and four daughters, the oldest being a daughter named Lucy. Lucy grew up during the American Revolution. During the years directly following the war Lucy became pregnant out of wedlock, and bore her child at the farm of Joseph Hanks in 1784. The tiny girl was named Nancy.

Just about this time the Hanks family pulled up stakes and moved westward to the far reaches of Virginia, now called West Virginia.

Lucy Hanks, unmarried, stayed in Virginia near the farm where the Hankses had lived. Records show that she was charged with fornication, but was never brought to trial. Meanwhile she had met a young man named Henry Sparrow. Apparently Sparrow took pity on her and married her. Lucy Hanks bore Sparrow nine children and made him a decent and pious wife, according to the records.

Whether Lucy renounced her illegitimate child, or whether the Hankses, ashamed of her actions, forced her to surrender her baby, is not known. Nancy Hanks became a ward of her grandfather and grandmother, traveling with the Hankses when they left Virginia.

They stayed in what is now West Virginia only about a year. Joseph sold the farm and they moved further westward to Kentucky. Little Nancy continued to live with the Hankses.

Joseph Hanks died when Nancy was about thirteen. Nancy's grandmother had never cottoned to Kentucky and moved back to Virginia. There Nancy was farmed out to live with an aunt, a sister of Lucy Hanks who had also married a Sparrow.

At her aunt's, Nancy learned the rudiments of her letters. She finally was able to read the Bible. However, she never did learn to write her own name. Eventually she was given room and board at the home of a family named Berry, where she acted as family seamstress.

During those years she met a young man named Thomas Lincoln. On June 10, 1806, they were married.

Thus Abraham Lincoln was legitimate, but his mother was not. Although the fact was not known widely during Lincoln's lifetime, it became the sensation of the country some years after his assassination.

So far as is known, Nancy Hanks was the only mother of a president of the United States who was illegitimate.

Though her heritage was shadowed, Nancy Hanks Lincoln enjoyed a relationship with her son that was certainly not as flawed as that between Thomas Jefferson and his mother or that between George Washington and his mother.

Thomas Jefferson was only fourteen years old when his father died. By that time the boy had become convinced that his father was a man much to be imitated and admired, but probably never equaled or surpassed. The older Jefferson was a strong role model for his talented son.

The same could not be said of Jefferson's mother. Jane Randolph had married Peter Jefferson in 1739. Her family had lived in Virginia for several generations, but Randolphs would occasionally return to England for business or personal reasons.

Her own father, Isham Randolph, was serving as colonial agent in London when he married an English girl in the early 1700s. Jane was born in the London parish of Shadwell in 1720. Shortly after her birth, Randolph sailed for America once again, where he became adjutant general of the Virginia Colony. Jane grew up in America.

When Peter Jefferson built a house for his new wife and growing family, he named it Shadwell, after the London parish in which Jane was born. He awarded her lifetime rights in Shadwell; that is, Jane Randolph Jefferson was entitled by law to live at Shadwell until she died, after which time it was to pass on to her oldest son, Thomas.

Unfortunately, Shadwell did not ever become her son's home. It was destroyed some time before her death by fire—a strange fire that was never satisfactorily explained. The blaze occurred in 1770, some years after Thomas Jefferson had been admitted to the Virginia bar. He had moved out of the house years before—ostensibly to make a life of his own, but subliminally, if we can believe all the stories, to get away from his mother.

Young Jefferson had decided to build a house for himself on a piece of land he had inherited. An architect and engineer, he had already drawn up plans for a large structure on the property—a place to be called Monticello.

Jefferson was supervising its construction and living on the building site at the time of the Shadwell fire. His younger sisters and brothers were living at Shadwell with his mother.

The story goes that a servant raced up to Monticello, woke him in the middle of the night, and told him the news that Shadwell had been completely gutted by fire.

The young man's first reaction was to ask about his books. He had left his rather large library there at home until he finished Monticello. Were his books safe?

No, they were gone, he was told. "But we saved your fiddle," the servant told him. Jefferson was an amateur musician who had learned to play the violin in his youth—and played it tolerably well.

It was only then, apparently, and as somewhat of an afterthought, that Jefferson thought to ask about his mother.

Oh, she was safe, he was informed.

However, it came out later that there was good reason to suspect that the fire had not occurred spontaneously; that it might, indeed, have been deliberately set.

There was some suspected mental instability in the Randolph family. About Jane Jefferson, a source once said, "She was crazy as can be. She tried to burn down that house three times, and finally she succeeded."

Jefferson wrote little about his mother. There was definitely no proof that she was a firebug. Certainly, however, he did spend a great deal of his life while she was still alive as far away from her as possible.

George Washington was another son who maintained as much distance from his mother as he could throughout his adult life. And she gave him good cause to be remote.

George was only eleven when his father died. Ferry Farm was left to George as the oldest boy of Augustine Washington and his second wife, to be legally his when he became twenty-one. George's mother, Mary Ball Washington, was left to bring up the rather large family by herself.

Mary Ball grew up in a family situation that was tangled and complex. For example, her father and her mother each married twice, and Mary was always in conflict with her stepbrothers and stepsisters. The complications that arose out of trying to split up the inheritance among the various siblings made her wary at an early age of property rights and the vagaries of dividing up the spoils.

In fact, she spent much of her youth in the home of a lawyer-relative, where she got first-hand knowledge of the wranglings and entanglements of the law.

She was contentious by nature, and by the time she took over the management of her growing family, she had developed into a truly opinionated, headstrong tyrant. Not only did she lord it over her own children, but also over the stepchildren of Washington's prior marriage.

As soon as he could, George moved out to live with his half brother Lawrence at Mount Vernon, the property Lawrence had inherited from his father. Although George visited the family on occasion, he spent as little time as possible there from that day on—at least while his mother was around.

Others in the family shared George's opinion of his mother's nature. One cousin once said of her: "Of the mother I was ten times more afraid than my own parents."

Mary Ball Washington did have one weakness: a pathological fear of lightning.

When she was a girl, she was seated at the dinner table next to a female friend. Lightning struck through the roof during a thunderstorm, killing the girl next to her instantly. The bolt was so hot it melted the knife and fork in the girl's hands, burning her body hideously.

Mary never recovered from the shock of this terrifying incident. On the approach of a thundercloud, she habitually retired to her own room, and would not leave it again until the storm had passed and the thunder and lightning ceased.

Other than lightning, she was afraid of little.

A contractor once failed to carry out her specific orders on a job he was hired to do. When she called his attention to instructions he had disregarded, he said that in his judgment he had done the work to more advantage than it would have been done by her directions.

She immediately checked him off. "And, pray, who gave you any exercise of judgment in the matter? I command you, sir; there is nothing left for you but to obey!"

She was rough even on those in her famly who tried to help her. When her son-in-law Colonel Fielding Lewis once proposed that he should help her in the management of her affairs, she shook her head and told him: "Keep my books in order, for your eyesight is better than mine. *But leave the executive management to me.*"

The strained relationship between George Washington and his mother was based on a simple scientific fact: likes repel and opposites attract. He was *too much like her* to get along with her, or to submit to her yoke. For months on end he would stay at either Lawrence's home at Mount Vernon, or at the home of his other stepbrother, Augustine.

Both his older half brothers had gone to school in England; when he asked his mother to send him away to study, she refused, pleading inability to manage it financially. She would accept no help for him from his stepbrothers.

Lawrence wanted him to join the navy when he was fourteen, but his mother resisted the idea. She wanted him to apprentice himself out to a tinker. A tinker was a mender of pots and pans, a low-class and nonprestigious job for a drifter or vagrant. Mary Washington was not one to think big.

Instead of becoming a sailor, George Washington went out to learn surveying, practicing the profession under his stepbrother Lawrence and Lawrence's father-in-law, Colonel William Fairfax. He worked for the colonel for several years, helping map out his extensive land holdings.

The Virginia militia was sent westward to fight off the French and Indians in 1748, and the young George joined up and found that the more distance he put between himself and his mother, the happier he was. Eventually the Indian troubles calmed down, and he returned home, where she once again tried to manipulate and dominate him.

To get away from her influence, he traveled with Lawrence to the West Indies in 1751. Shortly after their return, Lawrence died suddenly in 1752, and left the large estate at Mount Vernon to George. Thankfully, George moved there permanently, and continued to manage the two farms his mother insisted on holding for him.

When he turned twenty-one and technically became the full owner of Ferry Farm—where his mother and younger brothers and sisters were living—plus an adjoining farm facility nearby, she would not let him take possession of them. Instead she ordered him to manage both farms from his vantage point in Mount Vernon; he did so, visiting Ferry Farm as little as possible.

Mary continued living at Ferry Farm legally as a renter, never allowing her son to collect a penny from her. In fact, she extracted all the profits from the farm and let him have none of it. Their relationship consisted mostly of ugly wranglings over finances.

Every time he visited her she nagged him for money. In despair he took to visiting his married sister Betty—Mrs. Fielding Lewis—whenever he was near the old farm.

When he did succumb to guilt and visited his mother, he jotted down the name of any witness present when he handed her cash; this was an attempt to forestall her convenient lapses of memory. It was said she was extremely stingy in her own domestic affairs. She sometimes kept meat so long in her larder that she was obliged "to lean over her plate and smell each slice before conveying it to her mouth."

When he was twenty-three, Washington was asked by General Edward Braddock, head of the Virginia militia, to become his aide. The excessive bickering that took place between Washington and his mother, who did all she could to stop him from going, delayed the appointment temporarily. But Washington finally decided to ignore her wishes and agreed to join Braddock's staff as a colonel.

During the military campaign—once again against the French and Indians—Mary Washington began peppering her son with whining missives, pleading poverty. She wanted him to provide her with "a Dutch man"—a steward to run her farms (they were actually his farms). She also expected her son to procure fresh butter for her needs.

Washington responded testily from the wilderness of western Virginia, where butter was indeed a rarity:

"I am sorry it is not in my power to supply you with a Dutch man, or the butter as you desire, for we are quite out of that part of the country where either are to be, as there are few or no inhabitants where we now lie encamped, and butter cannot be had here to supply the wants of the camp."

She ignored his sarcasm and pleaded in her next letter for him to give up his command and come home to take care of her and the farm. He responded:

"If it is in my power to avoid going to the Ohio again, I shall, but if the command is pressed upon me by the general voice of the country, and offered on such terms as cannot be objected against, it would reflect eternal dishonor on me to refuse it; and that, I am sure, must, or ought, to give you greater cause of uneasiness than my going in my honorable command."

When Washington eventually married Martha Dandridge Custis, a widow, he was at the somewhat advanced age of twenty-seven. His mother was quite pleased that he was now settled down and would be unable to pursue his prospects in the military.

It was 1759 and Washington was living at Mount Vernon, away from the wars with the French. "Thear was no end of my troble while George was in the army," Mary crowed to a friend, "but he has now given it up."

For some years after that Mary Washington seemed to keep her mouth shut, but there was no question that she continued to hound her son for money, for food, and for other amenities. But George had pressing family problems to contend with and paid little attention to her. Apparently she realized he was ignoring her; she lay in wait for a long time when he might have less to do.

That time came in 1772. George's stepson had married and left the household, and once again Mary Washington appeared on the scene to become a nagging problem, like an aching tooth.

Badgered constantly now for money and assistance, George did not know what to do. He summed up his mother's financial situation this way:

"She has had a great deal of money from me at times, as can be made appear by my books . . . and over and above this has not only had all that was ever made from the plantation but got her provisions and everything else she thought proper from thence. In short, to the best of my recollection I have never in my life received a copper from the estate, and have paid many hundred pounds (first and last) to her in cash.

"However, I want no retribution; I conceived it to be my duty, whenever she asked for money, and I had it, to furnish her, notwithstanding she got all the crops, or the amount of them, and took everything she wanted from the plantation for the support of her family, horses, etc., besides."

In desperation, Washington then called a family council to decide what to do about mother. The powwow consisted of Jack Washington, George's favorite brother, and Betty Lewis, his favorite sister. Charles and Samuel were present, but hardly able to offer much help due to their own straitened circumstances.

Mary Washington was now sixty-three years of age, and seemed in excellent health in spite of her cries of misery. It was finally decided that the family would build her a house in Fredericksburg, a small cottage that would be within walking distance of her daughter Betty's house. George agreed to pay for the materials for the house, to supervise its construction, and to pay for its maintenance.

Mary had a turn of heart. She agreed to the idea. And in return for the house, Washington was finally able to wrest control of Ferry Farm and one other property from her, which had been his legally for many years. He sold them both for a handsome profit. At last, for a few years, his mother settled down close to her daughter Betty.

World history caught up with George Washington. After fifteen years of happiness at Mount Vernon, Washington was called, in 1774, to the first Continental Congress in Philadelphia. He stayed on to the second in 1775, and then on June 17 of that year he was appointed commander in chief of the armed forces of the United Colonies—which were now, quite suddenly, at war with England.

But Mary thought only of herself. "I never lived soe pore in my Life," she wrote in a querulous letter to her son Jack. "No Corn in the Corn House." She wanted help from him and from George both. And she said that if it was not for a neighbor and Betty, her daughter, she would be "almost starved." And then, in typical self-pitying style: "I am like an old almanac quite out of date."

But in 1781 a real blow fell on Washington. The army was faring badly, and was near total collapse. There was no money from Congress to fight the war. Much of Washington's own money had gone into the bottomless pit of the war, and he was almost destitute.

Mary cried poverty and destitution again. Her pleas did not go unheeded. Forces not particularly friendly to George Washington in the Virginia Assembly decided to make political hay out of her grievances. The assembly let it be known that plans were under way to grant her a pension at public expense to prevent her from starving. She was, they said, "in great want, owing to the heavy taxes she was obliged to pay."

Washington was at the end of his patience. He immediately wrote to a friend in Virginia, underlining his own doubts about his mother's poor-mouth utterances.

"True it is, I am but little acquainted with her *present* situation of distresses, if she is under any." He pointed out that she was living near her daughter Betty. "Before I left Virginia I answered all her calls for money; and since that period have directed my steward to do the same."

He was, he went on, appalled at the idea that his mother would become a pensioner, "or in other words," as he put it, "receiving *charity* from the public."

"Confident I am that she has not a child that would not divide the last sixpence to relieve her from *real* distress. This she has been repeatedly assured of by me; and all of us, I am certain, would feel most hurt at having our mother a pensioner while we had the means of supporting her; but in fact she has an ample income of her own."

Still simmering over his mother's actions, he wrote Jack.

"That she can have no *real* wants that may not easily be supplied I am sure of. *Imaginary* wants are indefinite; and often times insatiable, because they sometimes are boundless, and always changing. . . . If the rent is insufficient while I have anything I will part with it to make her so; and wish you to take measures in my behalf accordingly."

Apparently the Virginia Assembly drew back from its plans, and no pension was arranged.

In 1787 Washington was called to serve as president of the convention to adopt the U.S. constitution. Mary Washington was back to her old tricks of complaining bitterly about her problems. Washington had a solution.

"A man, a maid, the phaeton and two horses, are all you would want. To lay in a sufficiency for the support of these would not require ¼ of your income, the rest would purchase every necessity you could possibly want, and place it in your power to be serviceable to those with whom you may live, which no doubt would be agreeable to all parties. . . . By the mode I have pointed out you may reduce your income to a certainty, be eased of all trouble, and if you are so disposed, may be perfectly happy; for happiness depends more upon the internal frame of a person's own mind than on the externals of the world."

Their roles were reversed now, and Washington was giving lessons to his aged mother. But she was not to be assuaged. In 1788 she complained again, this time pleading for more cash. Washington dutifully sent her fifteen guineas and strongly advised her to give up the management of her little house. She was eighty years old now.

"My sincere and pressing advice to you is to break up housekeeping, hire out all the rest of your servants except a man and a maid and live with one of your Children. This would relieve you entirely from the cares of this world, and leave your mind at ease to reflect undisturbedly on that which ought to come. . . ."

In other words, he suggested that she rent out the land and house and go live with one of her children close by, most probably Betty, where her income would be enough for her wants. Then he continued, in the vein of the dutiful son, but with cautious overtones reserved to keep her from jumping immediately to the carrot held out.

"My house is at your service, & would press you most sincerely & devotedly to accept it, but I am sure, and candour requires me to say, it will never answer your purposes in any shape whatsoever, for in truth it may be compared to a well resorted tavern, as scarcely any strangers who are going from north to south, or from south to north do not spend a day or two at it.

"This would, were you to become an inhabitant of it, oblige you to do one of 3 things, 1st to be always dressing to appear in company, 2d, to come into [company] in dishabille or 3d to be as it were a prisoner in your own chamber. The first you would not like, indeed for a person at your time of life it would be too fatiguing. The 2d I should not like because those who resort here are as I observed before strangers and people of the first distinction—and the 3d, more than probably, would not be pleasing to either of us—nor indeed could you be retired in any room in my house; for what with the sitting up of Company; the noise and bustle of servants—and many other things you would not be able to enjoy that calmness and serenity of mind, which in my opinion you ought now to prefer to every other consideration in Life."

Mary Washington, needless to say, did not heed his advice, but stayed right where she was, complaining bitterly to the end to her daughter Betty. She died on August 25, 1789, of cancer of the breast, at the age of eighty-two.

She lived to see her son become president of the United States in 1788, although there is no indication of how she felt about that. She might have considered it simply another obstacle in the way of extracting more tribute and cash from her long-suffering son.

10

Threesome at the Bar Sinister

Of the forty presidents of the United States, only three of them apparently have been involved in siring children out of wedlock. One of these three was never clearly proven to be the father of the children ascribed to him, but the general opinion is that he too did have children out of wedlock.

Oddly enough, these three presidents come one to a century—one in the eighteenth, one in the nineteenth, and one in the twentieth.

Let's start with the more current playboy in the White House: Warren G. Harding. The child he sired out of wedlock was a daughter, and the girl's mother was Nan Britton. The story of her life appeared in 1927, four years after Harding's death. At the time of Harding's presidency, the fact of his illegitimate daughter was not known to the public at large, although there were rumors.

After the Nan Britton story came out, other stories began emerging about yet *another* mistress.

Harding was a successful newspaper publisher in Marion, Ohio, when he began his climb up the political ladder. He started out with two other partners in the ownership of the *Marion Star,* an ailing paper which the trio began to nourish and cultivate.

Eventually Harding gained controlling interest in the paper. Once he had done so, he began to solicit political advertising, and the *Star,* which had been an independent paper, became a Republican journal. It got all the Republican ads.

Harding now began to woo the daughter of the richest man in Marion. Amos Kling had made a mint of money in the hardware business. He was a whiz at real estate, too, parlaying his profits into a successful bank.

He had one daughter, Florence. Flossie Kling had been to the proper fashionable schools, and then to the Cincinnati Conservatory of Music. When she was nineteen years old, she ran away with Henry De Wolfe, a neighbor of Kling's. De Wolfe was a dissolute, a spendthrift, and an alcoholic. Kling was absolutely enraged.

The newly married De Wolfes had a baby boy six months after their marriage. Quite soon De Wolfe decided married life wasn't for him; he vanished. One story says that Flossie appealed to her father, who refused to give her one red cent. Another story claims that she was too proud to appeal to him at all. Whatever happened, she was destitute.

De Wolfe's father sent groceries to her and gave her shelter, if we are to believe one source; another says she was forced to stay with an unidentified friend. What *is* known is that she became a piano teacher on the strength of her training at the Conservatory of Music. When she was on her feet again, Kling relented and invited his daughter and grandson to live with him. He then adopted the boy and changed his name to Eugene Marshall Kling.

Flossie had been divorced ten years when she met Harding. He seemed a good catch for her. She was eight years older than he was, but she thought he might go places: He was a good-looking man with flowing hair, coppery skin, and a bluff hearty manner. And he owned the *Marion Star*.

She was a go-getter, and she went, and she got him. Her father was dead set against Harding. He did everything he could to break up the match, but he failed. They were married in 1891. Kling refused to speak to his daughter for seven years.

Flossie was a no-nonsense woman, a driving, forceful person, who knew all about business and how to run things. He took to calling her "The Duchess."

One day in the first years of his married life Harding stayed home sick. Flossie went down to the office and ran the *Star* while he recuperated. Harding decided that she was doing a better job than he was, and he stayed away, acting as a front man.

"I went down there intending to help out for a few days," she said, "and remained fourteen years."

Flossie, who knew how to pinch pennies, brought a sense of business to the enterprise. She organized a force of delivery boys and managed the advertising department, turning the paper into a real money-maker.

One of the *Star*'s most famous employees, next to Harding, who became a U.S. president, was Norman Thomas, who ran for president on the Socialist ticket six times—and lost every time. He didn't think much of Harding.

"Mrs. Harding in those days ran the show," he wrote. "Her husband was the front. He was, as you know, very affable; very much of a joiner and personally popular. He was a fine small-town or city booster."

Harding was doing as well politically as the paper was doing financially. By 1899 he was elected to the state senate, and reelected in 1901. Two years later he ran for lieutenant governor of Ohio, and won.

He was popular with his constituents—and popular as well with the ladies. In later years it was learned that Harding was always a ladies' man. While Flossie stayed home minding the store, he began a number of liaisons, two of which were, to say the least, sensational. The first of the two was with Carrie Phillips, the wife of James E. Phillips, a partner in the Uhler-Phillips department store in Marion. They became intimate when Harding was lieutenant governor of Ohio.

It apparently started when Flossie Harding was at a Columbus hospital and Phillips was in treatment at a Battle Creek hospital. While both spouses were away, Harding took up with Carrie. The affair lasted long after Flossie and Phillips returned to Marion—with letters between them dated between 1909 and 1920.

In fact, the Phillipses and the Hardings were very good friends. They toured the Mediterranean and Egypt together in 1909. Later on, they vacationed in Bermuda. Carrie is said to have once asked Harding if he would leave his wife for her; when he did not reply, she sailed away to Europe for three years.

In the interim Harding had an affair with another Marion woman: Nan Britton, who had worked on the *Marion Star* when she was a teenager. The daughter of a Marion physician, she carried the torch for Harding for years.

When Harding was elected to the United States Senate in 1914, he and Flossie moved to Washington, leaving the management of the paper to the hired hands. It was while in Washington that his relationship with Nan Britton was reestablished—by her. She was living in New York at the time, and asked him for help in getting a job.

According to one account, Harding visited her on one of his trips to New York and then saw her often in Washington. The relationship immediately heated up into an affair, with Harding seeing her regularly in Manhattan on a kind of commuter schedule. A daughter was born to her October 22, 1919, in Asbury Park, New Jersey, when she was twenty-three. She named the girl Elizabeth Ann Harding.

In that year Harding was suddenly in the news again as a favorite son from Ohio for the presidency. In December he announced his candidacy. It is said that Harding arranged for

Nan Britton to work as a clerk at the convention, and saw her several times after he was nominated for president.

In spite of several rumors about Harding's dissolute life, and in spite of the whispers that Harding's nomination was the result of numerous deals in smoke-filled rooms, he was elected on a campaign promise of a return to normalcy after the war excesses of the Wilson era. So in 1921 the president and First Lady opened up the White House—a welcome change after the battened-down appearance during the Woodrow Wilsons' last sequestered years. Flossie told the press she would like to be referred to as the "Duchess." She conducted a crowded social calendar.

"No president's wife in the memory of the capital has displayed such endurance," the *Washington Post* wrote.

Unfortunately, the First Lady's verve did not last. She became seriously ill in 1922, and was under the care of a Marion doctor.

During those days of the First Lady's absence, the president apparently slipped out of the White House many times to visit Nan Britton. According to witnesses, he would drop in at Evalyn Walsh McLean's house to visit her. It was said Evalyn simply ignored him.

A woman visitor once saw the president come by. "I think we should rise when the president enters," she told McLean.

"Tut, tut," Evalyn replied. "He doesn't *want* to be noticed."

In *The President's Daughter,* written by Nan Britton four years after Harding's death, the extent of the Harding-Britton affair was somewhat elaborated, with descriptions of intimacies even in the White House—particularly in a small clothes closet just off the anteroom of the president's office. "We repaired there many times in the course of my visits to the White House," Nan wrote, where they could and did "share kisses in safety."

The memoir even specified that their child was conceived during a liaison on a couch in Harding's Senate office!

When these revelations were made public, Alice Roosevelt Longworth had something to say about it, as might be expected: "My God! We have a president of the United States who doesn't even know *beds* were invented—and his campaign slogan was 'Back to Normalcy'!"

Although Harding knew of his daughter's existence, he apparently never did see her. He was obviously afraid the story would leak to the press. As for Nan, she was in France in 1923, when President Harding died on the West Coast.

She married a Swedish mariner in 1924, but the marriage broke up soon afterward, and Nan found herself in desperate financial straits.

Harding had once promised to look after her and his daughter "forever." So Nan returned to Washington to see if she could somehow locate this legacy he had promised to her. She failed, apparently because there was none.

Then Nan sought out Harding's two sisters, Miss Daisy Harding and Mrs. Heber Votaw. Daisy was sorry for Nan and gave her money—almost a thousand dollars. Meanwhile, Harding's younger brother, Dr. George T. Harding, heard what was happening. Suspecting blackmail, he prevented any further contact between his sister and Nan.

Then Nan made an attempt to convince Dr. Harding that her story was true, but she had no papers or proof of any kind that Harding had sired her child. In the book she related that Harding's brother had promised to help her, but that she had never been able to see Harding again in spite of the promise.

In 1931, after all the publicity caused by the book, Nan Britton sued for a share of Harding's estate, which was still being litigated in the courts. However, the court decided against her. In 1932 she produced another book, *Honesty in Politics,* in which photographs of the child appeared. They bore a striking resemblance to Warren G. Harding.

Harding never admitted that he was the father of an illegitimate child, but another president did. He was Grover

Cleveland, the country's twenty-second and twenty-fourth president.

Ironically enough, the *only* president to admit to a siring an illegitimate child was the son of a Congregational minister, graduated from Yale with honors, and trained in religion at Princeton! And his mother was a strict, ambitious, rigorously moral woman who taught her son never to settle for mediocrity of any kind or to allow himself any human weakness. So much for heritage.

His father died in 1853, when Cleveland was sixteen, and he immediately assumed the responsibility of supporting his mother and unmarried sisters, leaving him no time, energy, or money to marry and bring up a family of his own, until rather late in life.

Cleveland was admitted to the bar in 1859, and became a partner in the Buffalo law firm of Laning, Cleveland and Folsom. Oscar Folsom was Cleveland's best and closest friend.

In 1863 Cleveland became assistant district attorney for Erie County. He ran for district attorney in 1865, but was defeated. In 1872 he was elected sheriff of Erie County. And it was during his term as sheriff that he met a widower named Maria Crofts Halpin.

Maria was thirty-five; the sheriff was thirty-six at the time he met her. She was a tall, slender, and cultured woman. Maria had arrived in Buffalo in 1869 from New Rochelle, New York, with her husband and two children. When Halpin died in 1870, Maria sent her two children home to live with relatives in New Rochelle. Then she opened a collar-making shop, and later worked in a department store. The money she made in Buffalo went to support her children.

Sheriff Cleveland did not feel at the time that he could marry her, because of his responsibilities to his widowed mother. However, when the widow became pregnant Cleveland still did not marry her. On September 14, 1874, a child was born, baptized Oscar Folsom Halpin. Cleveland's law partner, Oscar Folsom, stood in at the baptism.

Soon after the baptism of her daughter, Maria Halpin began complaining that Cleveland had promised to marry her. He denied the charge. He said that he had promised to provide for her and the boy, and he was doing that, apparently by sending her money.

On July 23, 1875, Oscar Folsom was thrown from a buggy and killed almost instantly. He died without a will. Cleveland was made administrator of his estate. He made Folsom's young daughter, Frances, his ward, and sent money regularly to his partner's widow.

Meanwhile, the situation with Maria Halpin and Cleveland's baby boy worsened. Maria Halpin began drinking and neglecting the baby. When Cleveland heard what was happening, he visited her and pleaded with her to go easy on the alcohol. An argument ensued.

The baby was about a year and a half old when Cleveland began to worry about his safety at the hands of his hard-drinking mother. On March 9, 1876, he went to the office of the overseer of the poor, and spoke to an old political friend, John C. Level. He wanted Level to sign an order to take the child from its mother. The action was legal. She was unfit to care for him. Level signed.

Two police detectives arrived at the widow's apartment. When she learned they were there to take her child she fought with them, resisting physically. "It was a hell of a time," one of the detectives said.

But they removed the child to the Protestant Orphan Asylum, where he was boarded out at $5 a week. The widow was taken to the Providence Asylum, a hospital for alcoholics. She stayed five days.

Cleveland then gave her money to start up a business in Niagra Falls. She was granted permission to visit her child at the orphanage. Twice she visited her son. On April 28, she snatched the child and vanished with him.

Three months later the boy was recovered. The widow then wanted to sue Cleveland. Cleveland apparently paid her off to the tune of $500. Soon after that, the boy was legally adopted by an eminent Buffalo family of Cleveland's acquaintance. Eventually he became "a distinguished professional man," in the words of biographer Allan Nevins.

The widow moved back to New Rochelle and lived with her children and an aunt for a while, and then married again.

In 1882 Cleveland's mother died. In her own way this pious woman had ingrained such a sense of responsibility into her fifth child that she had indirectly caused him to violate one of the strongest tenets of her religious morality.

Cleveland's brief tenure as mayor of Buffalo in 1882 brought him a great deal of public acclaim; that same year he was elected governor of New York. Two years later he was nominated by the Democrats at their convention in Chicago for the presidency.

And the story of his illegitimate child by Maria Halpin broke in the press. One biographer wrote: "It was the saddest of ironies that if he had felt free to marry, this intensely moral man would almost certainly not have fathered the illegitimate child whose existence came to light when he was running for President."

Cleveland refused to deny the truth. The Republicans began to nag him in torchlight parades and street rallies singing the following song:

Ma, Ma, where's my pa?
Ma, Ma, where's my pa?
Going to the White House!
Ha, ha, ha!

And the Democrats came right back:

Hurrah for Maria! Hurrah for the kid!
I voted for Cleveland,
And I'm damned glad I did!

In spite of the scandal, Cleveland won the election with a very narrow victory in the popular vote. It was apparently his refusal to lie about his illegitimate son that made him president.

On June 2, 1886 Cleveland married his ward, Frances Folsom, and eventually had five legitimate children. After suffering defeat in his first bid for reelection, he was returned to the White House to serve a second term in 1893.

There is really no proof at all that Thomas Jefferson was the father of five children out of wedlock by a quadroon slave girl. However, there were so many stories and printed material by witnesses that his liaison with Sally Hemings simply cannot be denied.

In 1772, at the advanced age of twenty-eight, Jefferson married Martha Wayles Skelton, a widow, and had six children by her, two of whom grew to maturity. When she died after ten years of marriage, Jefferson was sent to France by President Washington to undertake diplomatic chores.

He took his oldest daughter with him, along with James Hemings, a quadroon slave who cooked for him. Martha, called Patsy, was twelve at the time. After some time in Paris, Maria, called Polly, joined the family in Paris. Along with Polly came Sally Hemings, another of Jefferson's quadroon slaves.

Sally, like Tom, was the daughter of Betty Hemings, a mulatto. Betty took the name of her white father, John Hemings, an English sea captain. Her mother was a full-blooded slave owned by John Wayles.

Betty apparently became John Wayles's mistress, producing three children—Sally, James, and John. But John Wayles was legitimately married, and one of his daughters was Martha Wayles, who married Thomas Jefferson after the death of her first husband.

Thus, Sally Hemings, a mixed-blood, was Martha Wayles's half sister. In fact, when Martha's father, John Wayles, died, Martha Jefferson inherited his passel of slaves. Among them were the Hemings brood. Sally was one-quarter black—a quadroon—as were her brothers, James and John.

In Paris Jefferson had two servants—Sally Hemings and her brother James. James did Jefferson's cuisine. Both Jefferson daughters were sent to a convent for their schooling.

Although not Catholics, they were accepted like many other Protestants in the school.

Sally was an extremely pretty girl, with an infectious manner and a commanding presence. At the time of Sally's arrival with his daughter Polly, Jefferson was involved in a complex and doomed romantic affair with a woman named Maria Cosway. She was married to an English fop and dilettante who engaged in indiscriminant sordid extramarital affairs with both women and men.

The affair had just broken up when Sally arrived. She seemed to fill the bill. Jefferson, it was said, had made a promise on his wife's deathbed never to marry again. But in the mores of the Paris in which he was then living, there was nothing against cohabitation.

The story goes that he took Sally more or less on the rebound from his shattered affair with Maria Cosway. Sally became pregnant. Jefferson's daughters suspected something, and became obstreperous. When, in April 1789, Patsy told her father she wanted to become a Catholic nun, Jefferson knew she was simply getting back at him for his freedom with Sally. So he yanked his daughters out of the convent and they spent the rest of their time in Paris in their hotel suite.

In France, both James and Sally Hemings were technically free; the French system, in the throes of the Revolution, did not recognize slavery. Jefferson knew he would have to be leaving for America soon enough. But Sally would have none of it. She was free; he could not force her to return to America and slave status on the plantation. Jefferson apparently promised freedom to her and her brother—*and* to the child Sally would produce.

Then he quickly packed up and the entourage sailed for the United States. When they arrived at Monticello, Sally Hemings gave birth to a little boy. The child was named Tom.

According to most sources, although there is actually no proof in existence, Sally Hemings bore Jefferson five children in all. The first, Tom, conceived in Paris and born at Monticello, either died as an infant or grew up free, apparently manumitted by Jefferson as he had promised Sally. Tom's name was not recorded in the Monticello farm books as a slave. The supposition is that he left the Jefferson estate around 1802 when the Sally Hemings scandal came to light, published by Jefferson's enemies.

Jefferson's grandson, Thomas Jefferson Randolph, son of Jefferson's daughter Patsy and Thomas Mann Randolph, Jr., once said of Sally: "She had children which resembled Mr. Jefferson so closely that it was plain that they had his blood in their veins." He went on to say that on one occasion a guest who was dining with Jefferson happened to glance quickly from the face of Jefferson to one of the black servants behind him and was astounded to see the close resemblance between master and servant. The resemblance was "obvious to all."

Henry S. Randall, a Jefferson biographer, wrote: "In one case the resemblance was so close, that at some distance or in the dusk the slave, dressed in the same way, might have been mistaken for Mr. Jefferson."

In addition to Tom, four other children were borne by Sally Hemings, apparently by Jefferson. They were Beverly, Madison, Eston, and Harriet—three sons and one daughter.

In 1873 Madison Hemings wrote his reminiscences, and in them stated that he was Thomas Jefferson's son by Sally Hemings. The manuscript described Jefferson's trip to Paris.

" [Jefferson] had had sons born to him, but they died in early infancy, so he then had but two children—Martha and Maria. The latter was left at home, [on the trip to Paris] but was afterwards ordered to follow him to France. She was three years or so younger than Martha.

"My mother [Sally Hemings] accompanied her as her body servant. When Mr. Jefferson went to France Martha was a young woman grown, my mother was about her age, and Maria was just budding into womanhood. Their stay [Sally's and

Maria's] was about eighteen months. But during that time my mother became Mr. Jefferson's concubine, and when he was called back home she was *enceinte* by him.

"He desired to bring my mother back to Virginia with him but she demurred. She was just beginning to understand the French language well, and in France she was free, while if she returned to Virginia she would be re-enslaved. So she refused to return with him.

"To induce her to do so he promised her extraordinary privileges, and made a solemn pledge that her children should be freed at the age of twenty-one years."

They did return, Madison continued. "Soon after their arrival, she gave birth to a child, of whom Thomas Jefferson was the father."

And, "She gave birth to four others, and Jefferson was the father of all of them. Their names were Beverly, Harriet, Madison [myself] and Eston—three sons and one daughter. We all became free agreeable to the treaty entered into by our parents before we were born."

The manuscript continued with a rundown of what happened to the offspring of Sally Hemings: According to Madison's version of the story, Tom, the son whom Sally bore shortly after returning to the United States, was declared to have died shortly after birth. (Other sources claimed he vanished in 1802 and passed for white elsewhere in the country.)

Beverly, born in 1798, left Monticello in 1822 and passed as a white man in Washington. He was married in Maryland to a white woman, and had a daughter; no one guessed that she had any black blood.

Harriet, born in 1801, passed for white in Washington City and married a white man. She raised a family of children, none of whom suspected their origins in Monticello.

Eston, born in 1808, married a black woman in Virginia then moved on to Ohio, and lived in Chillicothe for several years. He later went up to Wisconsin, where he died, leaving three children.

Madison, born in 1805, married a woman whose grandmother was a slave, and then moved on to Ohio in 1836. He was a carpenter. Madison died in 1877, shortly after writing about his early life at Monticello and naming Jefferson as his father.

Another Jefferson slave, Israel Jefferson, also published *his* reminiscences in 1873, including details about the private life of Thomas Jefferson.

For fourteen years, he wrote, he made the fire in Jefferson's bedroom and private chamber, dusted his books, cleaned his office, and did everything needed.

"I know that it was a general statement among the older servants at Monticello, that Mr. Jefferson promised his wife, on her death bed, that he would not again marry. I also know that his servant, Sally Hemmings (mother to my old friend and former companion at Monticello, Madison Hemmings), was employed as his chamber-maid, and that Mr. Jefferson was on the most intimate terms with her; that, in fact, she was his concubine."

But biographer Henry S. Randall suggested that Peter Carr and Samuel Carr, the sons of Jefferson's sister Martha and Dabney Carr, were actually the fathers of Sally's children, *not* Jefferson. Randall wrote that Jefferson's grandson Thomas Jefferson Randolph told him that Sally Hemings was Peter's mistress and that Betsey Hemings, also called Beth, a half sister of Sally's, was Samuel's mistress.

"Both the Hening girls were light colored and decidedly good looking," Randall went on, misspelling the Hemings name each time with an *n* instead of an *m*, and without the *s*.

Randall quoted Randolph that "their connection with the Carrs was perfectly notorious at Monticello, and scarcely disguised by the latter—never disavowed by them. Samuel's proceedings were particularly open."

It was never explained how either Carr nephew got to Paris at the time Sally Hemings became pregnant.

Whether or not the five Hemings offspring were Jefferson's

or not remains unproved to this day. But many competent historians believe that they were indeed Jefferson's illegitimate offspring.

"If the story of the Sally Hemings liaison be true, as I believe it is," writes Fawn M. Brodie, "it represents . . . a serious passion that brought Jefferson and the slave woman much private happiness over a period lasting thirty-eight years."

And if it is true, it is the first example of such a large group of illegitimate children in a First Family.

11

Inlaws and Outlaws

While most of the offspring of presidents tend to marry well, some of them do not. Married life is a guessing game at best. When a son or a daughter of a chief executive makes a bad marriage, the repercussions may continue through many years. Other times the press may be bad for only a short time, but with serious results.

John Tyler, tenth president of the United States, was married twice, and during the course of his two marriages produced fifteen children, fourteen of whom grew to maturity. And almost all of them married. The odds were, certainly, that at least one of his children might marry someone of less than ordinary repute.

Tyler's fourth child was a girl, named Letitia after her mother, Tyler's first wife.

Several years before Tyler became president—he served

from 1841 to 1845—Letitia was married to James A. Semple, the nephew of a prominent Williamsburg, Virginia, judge and the heir to a substantial fortune.

Tyler approved the marriage. His new son-in-law was a near neighbor on the James River. His daughter was known as "very handsome, full of life and spirits," the perfect mate for the young Southern aristocrat. The couple settled at Cedar Hill plantation in New Kent County. A marriage of harmony, prosperity, and happiness seemed assured.

During Tyler's third year as president he secured a commission for Semple as a purser in the U.S. Navy. For the next decade and a half, Semple spent most of his time at sea or on duty in his navy officer's job. But when the Civil War broke out, and his father-in-law had long left Washington, he resigned his commission and went with the South.

He never really accepted the South's surrender. He became the stereotype of the unreconstructed Southerner, a man apt to mutter that "the South shall rise"—a kind of fantasy-ridden Ashley Wilkes, unable to accept the downturn of his own fortunes and the end of the Southern aristocracy of which he was a proud member.

Letitia Semple was a product of the same society as her husband, but there was a hard core of reality in her nature. She could not understand why her husband could not adjust to defeat. Their marriage had been in trouble almost from the day it began, and by the end of the Civil War it was almost totally in shambles.

Semple fled the postbellum South where Northern Reconstruction was taking place. At the time Canada was a hotbed of confused and dissident ex-Confederates. Semple became a unifying force working among them, trying to weld various expatriate groups into a fighting army, to return home and wrest the South from Northern hands.

In 1866, the year after hostilities had ceased, Semple returned to Alabama, in an underground capacity, trying to elect his brother-in-law, Robert Tyler, another unreconstructed rebel, to office in Alabama. He became involved in an abortive attempt to get Jefferson Davis out of prison, where he was held at Fortress Monroe.

These romantic efforts were doomed to failure from the start. But Semple had made a name for himself among the unorganized expatriates; eventually he became a kind of liaison man, propagandist, and secret agent for a certain Confederate Committee of Correspondence (CCC) carrying communications of insurrection and agitation between Canada and the South.

When the United States proposed the amnesty oath for all expatriated Confederates, Semple refused to join the Union and went underground as an agent for the CCC. He changed his name. His first alias was John Doe. But finally he became Allan S. James.

"James" actually assumed a physical disguise to differentiate himself from his old image; he became a cloak-and-dagger operative in the usual sense of the word. One of his most important fellow travelers in this subversive activity was his step-mother-in-law, the former First Lady, Julia Gardiner Tyler.

There had always been splendid rapport between Tyler's second wife and Semple. They were almost of a similar age. Besides that, Letitia's brother John Tyler, Jr. had been among Julia Gardiner's beaux at the White House before his father beat him out in the matrimonial sweepstakes.

When Julia Gardiner and the president married, most of the Tyler children accepted their stepmother without reservation. Letitia was the one holdout. She may have been jealous of her husband's open admiration for the new First Lady. As Letitia's marriage continued to disintegrate over the years, her husband often sought solace and advice from the First Lady.

But with their age difference so slight, it must have seemed to Letitia that her husband viewed her stepmother in a light quite different from that of elderly counselor. A romantic triangle developed.

In the postwar years, with Semple needing some kind of "safe house" for his spy activities, Julia Tyler, who had moved to New York during the war, filled the bill admirably. His former confidante now became his aide in espionage, proof, perhaps, that Julia always believed more in friendship than in political alliances.

Julia needed him as much as he needed her. Her stepdaughter Elizabeth Tyler Waller (from Tyler's first marriage) had married into the house of Jefferson Davis when she became the bride of William Nevison Waller during her father's presidency in Washington. Their son, William Waller, at West Point when the Civil War started, had resigned his commission to go with the Confederates.

During the war young Waller married the youngest sister of Varina Davis, Jefferson Davis's wife. When the war ended, Julia tried to retain contact with Varina Davis in order to give support where it could help. She saw that Semple was the man for the job. Every time he went through New York on his way to and from Canada, he visited his mother-in-law and passed on information to and from Varina Davis.

By 1865 Letitia was sick and tired of her husband's half-baked, comic-opera espionage activities. In a stormy confrontation she walked out on him and moved to Baltimore, where she opened a private school for girls, called the Eclectic Institute.

Semple and Julia were thrown together more and more. As Allan S. James, he continued his courier activities, working with Southern sympathizers in Montreal. He was lucky; Union officials never caught up with him.

"So far I am free and have no fears," he wrote to Julia, "as I am pretty well by this time acquainted with my own powers of adroitness, courage, etc., and can provide pretty well for emergencies."

He was not a man to suffer from humility.

His work in Montreal was all for naught. The underground rebels were always at each other's throats. "There is the devil to pay among the 'tribe' here," he wrote Julia in 1866. "No one speaks to the other and I have heard the most astounding reports and been questioned by a member of the 'tribe' and had no hesitation in at once answering all questions in writing, and I tell you now that by my own volition I will never pass another word with one of the members here. . . . I shall write to Mrs. Davis and inform old Jeff of the circumstances. . . . At the same time, I am ready to engage in any matter which will further the interests of the South."

He had been working at his espionage job for a year and a half and was no nearer success than when he began. In addition, Union agents were starting to piece together the truth about Allan S. James. He had several narrow escapes, and was almost captured at least once on his trips through the United States.

The stress was beginning to tell on Semple. He was beginning to show signs of mental deterioration. Always a bon vivant, he had been a moderate drinker during his younger days, able to hold his own with his Virginia aristocrat peers, but now he was becoming a compulsive toper.

Not only alcohol, but women as well, became his solace during those bleak months following the defeat of the South. He accosted showgirls and squired various fancy women about, all in an attempt to assuage his own frustration and depression.

He barely recognized the difference between James A. Semple and Allan S. James anymore. His brother-in-law Tazewell Tyler saw him in New York "constantly around the theaters, traveling about the country with actresses, gallivanting them in Central Park."

Wine and women were not all; he went in for the entire cliché. He began gambling at cards, winning some and losing more. Luckily he had not quite exhausted his fortune yet. But he was living on the thin edge of self-destruction.

Now the world of fantasy merged with the world of reality. His reliance on his mother-in-law, Julia Tyler, and her reliance on him became a true sexual relationship to his unhinged mind.

"You are good, *I know*, and beautiful to my eyes, *but you are not mine!!*" he wrote her. "My love you know you have taken, one day share my lot . . . my Sister darling."

Julia knew he was half insane, but she was flattered at his attentions. "Why should I not regard you most tenderly?" she wrote him in a long letter. But then she warned him that they were never to be lovers. "I will become your mentor to guide you into the right path whenever there is danger of your needing [counsel]. Thus I am sure our *friendship* will be unmistakable."

Her rejection did not help Semple's ego.

Around November 1866, Jefferson Davis advised Semple that he would like him to visit Mississippi on a "confidential matter." What that matter pertained to was unspecified in the communication.

By then Semple had decided he would quit his endeavors to resuscitate the South. "I am tired of being hunted down," he wrote to Julia. He declined the mission of the former Confederate president. And Allan S. James was no more.

The decision was a difficult one. Semple's involvement in the game of cat-and-mouse, his "disguise," his assumption of a false name, his theatrical "contacts" and "disappearances" all had played havoc with his psyche. He went into a mental decline and appeared suddenly in New Orleans, drinking and gambling, even threatening suicide. He was rapidly coming apart.

Shortly after giving up his espionage role, Semple suffered a nervous breakdown. Julia gave sanctuary to the shattered man in New York and paid for his room and board all through 1867, while he slowly recovered a semblance of his former self.

When the suspicious Letitia discovered that Julia was constantly at the bedside of her husband, she was beside herself with rage. She had always hated Julia, who was as attractive as Letitia herself, and was now a fancied rival for her husband's affection.

She suspected that Julia and Semple were lovers. She told them as much. Both denied the charges.

"Your remarks relative to Mrs. T.," wrote Semple to her

during his recovery in July 1867, "are not worthy of a daughter of John Tyler. No matter what I may think of a lady, I rather think I would keep it to myself. I was suffering and Mrs. T. offered me a home (I have never had one before) and I accepted it and passed many pleasant hours there.

"As to your terms relative to her I throw them back with the scorn which they deserve, a lady as she is and always will be. As to 'carrying my name' to save it from disgrace, it is incredulous." Then, at the end of the long letter, he told her: "Take your own steps and resume your own name."

Letitia did so. Although there was never any official divorce, Letitia never lived with Semple again. She even instituted a legal fight later on with Julia over some family portraits Semple had saved from the estate during the Civil War.

Semple dropped out of sight once he had regained his sanity in 1867. In 1870 he got a job with the York Railroad Company at Turnstalls Station in New Kent County, Virginia, near where he was born.

Some ten years later he visited Julia Tyler in Richmond. He was reported to be "looking so well." He had, he reported, been in Mexico helping the Revolutionary Porfirio Díaz overthrow the Establishment. He looked "quite a Mexican with mustache and large beard," she wrote.

Letitia died in 1907, at the age of eighty-six, in Baltimore. The date of Semple's death is not known.

Although James Monroe's two daughters managed to keep a personal feud between them going for most of their adult lives, it was really a son-in-law of the fifth president of the United States who was responsible for their animosity.

He was Samuel Lawrence Gouverneur, a nephew of the First Lady, Elizabeth Kortright Monroe. He had started out his career as a private secretary to President Monroe in the White House. There he met the president's younger daughter, Maria.

Monroe was actually closer to his older daughter. Elizabeth

was always called Eliza, and had been named for her mother. Eliza was born in 1786; Maria in 1803. They were seventeen years apart, and a gap separated them from the beginning.

Eliza was tall, quiet, and dark, with soft black eyes and glossy black hair. Maria Hester was blonde, bouncy, and lively—the mirror opposite of her older sister.

The cool one, Eliza, had been educated at one of the most famous of all French schools for girls, Madame Campan's, where she was enrolled at the age of seven during her father's first visit to France. She remained there until after graduation. Eliza was a lifelong friend of Hortense de Beauharnais, the stepdaughter of Napoleon; Hortense later became the queen of Holland.

Shortly after Eliza's return to America at the age of twenty-one, she married George Hay, an attorney who made his reputation prosecuting Aaron Burr on a charge of treason.

When Monroe became president in 1817, Hay was appointed a White House secretary. Eliza became a stand-in hostess for her mother. Because of her aristocratic upbringing, Eliza was a standoffish, snobbish, hard-to-get-along-with young lady. She favored royalty, was domineering in her lofty social decrees about protocol, and had a talent for making enemies everywhere she went.

She refused to attend any parties given by members of the diplomatic corps, a stand that was taken as an insult by all diplomats and their wives. Nor would she allow herself to be accorded any special mark of attention as the daughter of the president.

However, she did expect respect because of her husband's so-called social position, which according to her, originated with Hay's father. Although he was in truth only the owner of the Raleigh Tavern in Williamsburg, she pointed out that he was the younger son of England's Earl of Errol.

Washington society hated to see this member of the First Family wielding so much influence in the White House. In Louisa Adams's words, she was so "full of agreeables and disagreeables, so accomplished and ill bred, so proud and so mean," and so loved scandal, that no one's name was safe in her hands. A complicated lady.

Washington saw Eliza almost as much as they saw the First Lady, a more passive type who let her daughter run things. Eliza's way was the Continental way, not the American way. Neither of the two made any overt attempt to make or return social calls, and they were most selective about the calls they did make.

Finally they established a weekly "at home" in the White House, and helped out with the "required" office parties. But that was simply *not* the way it was done. Distaff Washington was annoyed. To a woman it boycotted the at-home affairs and stayed away in droves from the office parties given by wives of the cabinet members.

This caused a horrendous social flap in the nation's capital.

Typical of the acrimony of Eliza's tongue was her outburst one evening when her husband was away in Richmond on business. Several people came up to her asking where her husband was, and she dutifully replied that he was in Richmond.

But the question kept arising with each new arrival. Finally Eliza could put up with it no longer.

"How is Mr. Hay? And where is he?" a guest asked her.

"He's dead!" snapped Eliza. "I have just got the news. He's dead! And buried!"

In spite of her tart tongue, she was a kindhearted woman when she wanted to be. But her pride and her vanity stood in the way of many relationships she might have enjoyed with her contemporaries.

In contrast, her sister, Maria Hester, was completely sociable and friendly. She was not French-educated. She was brought up in Washington during the years when her father was secretary of state under President Madison.

Maria met Samuel Gouverneur when he was working for her father. They became engaged when she was sixteen and he twenty-one.

In her typically take-charge fashion, Eliza made all the marriage plans for her sister. Her ideas of protocol—dictated by exclusivity and rank in the European fashion—were quite foreign to American ideas of a big brassy exciting wedding knee-deep in presents, people, relatives, and spectators.

A disaster was in the making. News of Maria's engagement leaked out. Diplomats hoped the wedding would make for better White House relations. When their representatives called on the First Lady, she referred them to Eliza. Eliza snootily informed them that her sister could not receive and return their visits.

The wedding, she informed them, would be in what she called the "New York style," with only relatives and a few close friends of the family present. There would be seven bridesmaids and seven groomsmen. "Take no notice of the marriage," she told them.

There were only forty-two guests at the wedding dinner, when a White House wedding usually had five hundred! Maria and Gouverneur were married in the East Room of the White House on March 9, 1820, in a ceremony that was almost totally exclusive—in short, they were married almost alone. There were practically no presents! The wedding of Maria Hester and Samuel L. Gouverneur was conviviality in reverse.

After the wedding was over, the newlyweds went on a honeymoon trip to Virginia, and returned to attend a series of balls and receptions which had been planned for them. However, only one was actually held.

The death of an American hero, Commodore Stephen Decatur, who died of wounds received in a duel, caused all the rest to be canceled.

Gouverneur knew what had happened. He knew whom to blame. So did Maria. He *never* forgave Eliza.

From that time on, both families—the Hays and the Gouverneurs—communicated little. The break became complete some years later; none of the members of either branch associated with members of the other.

Maria's first child, named James Monroe Gouverneur, after her father, was born in the White House in 1822, and christened soon after that. Some months later he was discovered to be deaf, which turned the joy over his birth to unhappiness.

By now Gouverneur decided that the White House was not the place to live. He had his sister-in-law to contend with and he had the added misfortune of his handicapped child. He moved to New York with his wife and child, to live near his own parents. There Gouverneur's other two children were born, both normal.

Monroe served two terms as president, and when he left Washington he moved to Oak Hill, in Virginia, where he had built a home while president. The Gouverneurs were established in New York, but the Hays did not want to remain in Washington. They followed Eliza's father to Oak Hill.

Meanwhile, the Gouverneurs seemed to be struggling along without notable success. Monroe busied himself with his contacts in Washington, and finally persuaded friends to get his son-in-law the postmastership of New York City.

The lucrative position lasted until Andrew Jackson took office in 1829. Then, after a short but vindictive quarrel with Gouverneur over something his then-dead father-in-law said, the president dismissed him from the post.

In 1830, five years after Monroe left the White House, Eliza Hay's husband died. The former First Lady died the same year. The former president took that opportunity to move to New York to live with the Gouverneurs. He was there with them when he died in 1831.

Eliza Hay and the Gouverneurs still did not speak to one another. Eliza had always been considered her father's favorite. That was apparently why he had put her in charge of running Oak Hill. But when he was living with the Gouverneurs in New York, something happened.

Monroe's will left Oak Hill not to Eliza, who was living there and who had been taking care of it ever since her father had left to move to New York, but to his younger daughter Maria!

To add salt to the wound, Monroe left Eliza "to the fraternal care and protection of my son-in-law, Samuel L. Gouverneur"! He explained in his will that the reason he had left Oak Hill to Maria was that he had already given another estate, Ashfield, to Eliza; that would even up the property settlement. The rest of his property would be divided up between his two nonspeaking daughters.

Monroe left his presidential papers to his son-in-law in New York. Gouverneur had apparently said he would be interested in editing and publishing them. Eliza was to get one-third of any profit that resulted from their publication; Maria and her husband would each get one-third.

Gouverneur, never much of a businessman, and unchanged from his earlier days, was now a bon vivant and big-spending man-about-town. He thought about working on Monroe's papers, but when it came right down to it, he couldn't be bothered fussing with the effects of his has-been father-in-law. He let the editing assignment slide by, and did nothing. For Maria and Eliza there was no one-third profit from their publication.

Ironically, it was Eliza who had the last word in the family feud. She sailed for France to visit her childhood friend Hortense de Beauharnais. While there, she renounced her Protestant faith and became a Roman Catholic, with Pope Gregory VI converting her while she and Hortense were in Rome.

Eliza spent her last days in a convent. She died and was buried in Paris, like many other exiles before and after.

Maria and her family lived in New York and then moved down to Virginia to take possession of Oak Hill. Gouverneur was now more than a man-about-town—he was a gambling fool. The story went that Maria was forced to hide the family silver to keep him from pawning it to pay off his betting debts.

When visitors were expected one day at Oak Hill, Gouverneur was heard to call out to his son in a frantic voice: "For God's sake, have your mother get the silver out. We're going to have guests!"

Maria died before her do-nothing husband. In her will she left Oak Hill to him. He remarried and willed everything he had at his death to his second wife, thus cutting off the true Monroe descendants from any of the property. Oak Hill to this day is in private hands.

The Hatfields and McCoys could have learned a lot from these two headstrong Monroe women. And Gouverneur was no referee; he was more like a tournament director with all his money on a side bet.

Thomas Jefferson didn't have much more luck with his inlaws than he had with his own blood kin. Thomas Mann Randolph, Jr., was the son of Jefferson's cousin Thomas Mann Randolph, Sr., with whom he had been close friends and even lived with in his youth.

During Jefferson's stay in Paris with his two daughters, this second cousin dropped in for a short visit after graduating from the University of Edinburgh. He fell in love with Jefferson's daughter Martha (Patsy), and she with him.

Too soon, Randolph had to sail for home. However, in a short time, all the Jeffersons followed. Randolph and Patsy were married three months after the Jefferson entourage had reached Virginia.

Randolph was definitely a "catch"—tall and strong like his father-in-law—"brilliant, versatile, eloquent in conversation when he chose to be," and also an excellent outdoorsman and horseman, according to biographer Randall.

Jefferson called him "a young gentleman of genius, science, and honorable mind." He approved of the marriage. "I scrupulously suppressed my wishes that my daughter might indulge her own sentiments freely, but [Randolph's] talents, dispositions, connections and fortune were such as would have made him my own first choice."

Yet there was a darker side to Randolph's nature, a side that was not apparent to the Jeffersons at the time. Another observer with somewhat sharper perception described him as "impetuous and imperious in temper," and apt to be moody and hard to get on with. A swarthy, dark, handsome man with flashing eyes, Randolph was fond of bragging that the blood of Pocahontas flowed in his veins.

When Patsy and Randolph were married in February 1790, Jefferson provided a dowry of 1,000 acres of woodland and twenty-five slaves. Randolph's father gave the couple a plantation at Varina, Virginia.

From the beginning, it seemed the marriage had everything going for it. But very shortly it became evident that there was something fundamentally flawed in Randolph's complex character and makeup. There had always been a strain of instability in the Randolphs which has already been explored: in Jefferson's own mother, Jane, in Jefferson's sister, Elizabeth, and his brother Randolph. Apparently it lurked as well in the psyche of this Randolph.

On the surface things were going very well indeed. In the macho fashion of the time, Randolph kept his wife almost continually pregnant. Between 1790 and 1818 she bore him twelve children, of whom eleven survived childhood. But there were submerged drives within her husband that she had not dreamed of when she agreed to marry him.

Within months of their marriage, Randolph began experiencing sudden surges of incoherent anger, flaming rages, and mental aberrations that frightened his wife and drove her into panic. Brought up in a most tranquil atmosphere of love and respect, Patsy found these personal outbursts and threats of violence against her person incomprehensible.

Four years after they were married, Randolph's short outbursts and flights of fancy grew into much more serious and more prolonged manic highs and depressive lows. During his depressions, he would frequently threaten suicide. Sometimes he would give way to a sudden rage, perhaps directed at Patsy or at one of his children, and then he would hurl himself out of the house, mount his horse, and thunder off through the woods, trying to work off the emotional hyperactivity that suffused his entire personality.

"Darkness, the swollen ford, the rushing river, the wildly

beating storm, stopped not his journey when his horse's head was pointed homeward," wrote Jefferson's biographer Henry S. Randall about Randolph in the flowery prose of the time. "The tall spare figure wrapped in a horseman's cloak, the blazing but abstracted eye, the powerful blood-horse, splashed with mud and foam, and dashing swiftly onward, are yet familiar objects in the recollections of many."

His breakdowns were suppressed from the public, but Randolph's father-in-law knew enough about mental illness from the tragic experience of his sister Elizabeth to know that they were serious attacks indeed.

It never helped Randolph's equanimity to realize that his own father-in-law stood in his wife's eyes as an eternal symbol of superiority and prestige that he could never possibly equal. When Randolph visited Monticello he wrote that he felt quite like a "proverbially silly bird" who could never feel completely at ease among the swans.

Without quite understanding what she was doing, Patsy helped to unsettle her already disturbed husband by always deferring first to her father and becoming a satellite circling about him.

Nor was Randolph able to succeed at the one thing that Jefferson continually failed at—finances. Although the couple was well off, considering the number of slaves owned and the land possessed, Randolph never seemed to have enough money for Patsy to run the house. The hard-pressed Jefferson had to lend them over twelve hundred pounds in 1795.

At this time, Randolph's manic-depressive psychosis had progressed to an alarming degree, in fact, to an almost total disintegration of his character. He sought medical aid, but little was then known of mental illness. He went from one doctor to another, with not one of them able to prescribe any kind of treatment for his ailment.

His search for the right doctor consumed a great deal of money. There was simply not enough of it to cover the family budget. Jefferson took in Randolph's two children at Monticello and Patsy's sister Maria (Polly) offered to baby-sit the children while Patsy went around with her husband from doctor after doctor, searching out a cure.

Randolph's ego, never too robust, seemed completely shattered by his inability to care for her and his children without the help of his father-in-law, whom he resented.

Then, quite suddenly, his fortunes changed. In 1797 Jefferson was elected vice-president and moved to New York. Randolph's spirits rose almost immediately. His mental depression vanished.

He even ran for office as a delegate to the Virginia legislature. However, in typically Randolph fashion, he did not follow up his rather effective campaign on election day; in fact, he was not present during the election itself. Later on he said that his children had just been inoculated for smallpox and that he had been forced to stay home to help nurse them. In any event, he lost the election. He also lost a great deal of support by not showing up on that crucial day.

He received a note of recrimination from Jefferson, who said he felt his son-in-law's actions had personally humiliated him. He even sent letters of apology for Randolph's actions "to every militia captain" whom Jefferson knew. "I am more anxious you should possess the affections of the people than you should make use of them. Their esteem will contribute much to your happiness: whether the office they might confer would do so is another question."

Needless to say, his father-in-law's blast didn't sit well with Randolph.

Three years later Randolph was so broke he tried to borrow money from the vice-president. Jefferson could not oblige him; he had been handling the estate of a law client and had discovered an error he had made in repayment of money he had borrowed. To rectify the error, he had been forced to mortgage 1,000 acres of his own property.

He told Randolph what had happened. Whether or not Randolph sympathized hardly mattered; he did not get the money. It was a bad blow. A further bad blow was his father-in-law's elevation that very same year to the highest office in the land—president of the United States.

With Jefferson's great success as chief executive in the nation's capitol, Randolph's self-esteem sank even lower. In 1802 he had about had it with Virginia. He decided to pull up stakes and move to Mississippi to raise cotton. It took all Jefferson's persuasion to keep him from going.

Meanwhile, the president needed his two daughters at the capital to help with the many parties and dinners he had to give. Both Patsy and Polly left for Washington in 1802; Randolph stayed at Monticello taking care of the children. Being baby-sitter for seven growing kids could not have been good medicine for his pride. His animosity toward his father-in-law continued to grow, smouldering within him.

One reaction to what he considered his family's attempts to castrate and destroy him was to run for office again. In 1802 he became a congressional representative from his district. He never told the president he was going to run; and when he ran he defeated a very close friend of Thomas Jefferson's.

The defeated candidate immediately challenged the election results, claiming that there were irregularities in the proceedings and hinting that Randolph had somehow rigged the voting.

It took a congressional committee five months to decide whether or not he could even assume his seat. Nepotism was an issue too. Not an unheard-of thing in those days, it was then beginning to be hunted down and rooted out in Washington.

In Randolph's election, the relationship between the president and the candidate was a very close one by marriage. The congressional committee was full of Jefferson's enemies who would have loved to see the president humiliated. Jefferson himself was displeased with the complication. He had to expend energy and good will placating the defeated candidate whom Randolph had beaten.

Polly's husband, Jack Eppes, also won election to Congress the same year. Jefferson insisted both his sons-in-law live with him in the president's house. Once again Randolph found himself being measured against a better man. Everyone liked Eppes; no one seemed taken by Randolph. Randolph's own daughter Ellen once described her Uncle Jack as "a gay, good-natured, laughing man." She thought her father cold and austere. Trouble was beginning to brew between the two men confined under one roof away from home.

But it was not Eppes who took the brunt of Randolph's explosive attack when it came, but another kinsman, John Randolph of Roanoke, whose brother Richard had been married to Randolph's sister Judith. The quarrel began in Congress itself. Randolph denounced his kinsman as "bankrupt forever as a popular statesman."

The press immediately pounced on the outburst, and news stories hinted at a duel. Jefferson was beside himself. The president's son-in-law in an illegal duel! He tried to dissuade his daughter's moody husband.

"How different is the stake which you two would bring into the field!" he wrote Randolph. "On his side, unentangled in the affections of the world, a single life, of no value to himself or others, on yours, yourself, a wife, and a family of children, all depending for their happiness and protection in this world on you alone."

He pictured what would happen if Randolph was killed. "Seven children, all under the age of discretion and down to infancy could then be left without guide or guardian but a poor broken-hearted woman, doomed herself to misery the rest of her life. And should her frail frame sink under it, what is then to become of them? Is it possible that your duties to these dear objects can weigh more lightly than those to a gladiator?"

Somehow Randolph managed to make temporary peace between himself and his kinsman, but during Jefferson's second term took umbrage at something his brother-in-law Jack Eppes said regarding the disposition of his dead wife's property. Polly Eppes had died in 1804. Mostly Randolph was nursing his old grievances that Jefferson was favoring everyone else over him.

With both the quarreling kinsfolk under his roof, the president found himself in the role of arbitrator. A very poor arbitrator he was. Henry Adams, from his position of Monday morning quarterback, saw Jefferson as "not despotic in temper," but apt to display "to a certain degree the habits of a paternal despot."

In February 1807, there was a loud exchange between the two brothers-in-law, after which Randolph moved out of the White House and into a boarding house. He fired off an inflammatory letter to the president.

Jefferson's response was a cordial one: "I had for some days perceived in you a gloom which gave me uneasiness. I knew there was a difference between Mr. Eppes and yourself, but had no idea it was as deep seated as your letter shews it to be. I never knew the cause, nor ever wished to know it. My affections for you both were warm."

He assured Randolph that he had no preference for Jack Eppes over him, and if it seemed so, it was a mistake.

The letter did little to assuage Randolph's emotional state. He was in a suicidal mood. His old sickness of 1794 seemed to have taken hold of him once again, bringing on all kinds of rages and tantrums. Members of the boarding house into which he had moved tried to quiet him down. One of them, William Burwell, wrote in a letter to Thomas Jefferson: "Mr. R . . . observed he was indifferent to live . . . inspired with shame for having left you."

Senator William Plumer, a boarder with Randolph, noted that Randolph had a pair of pistols and a sword in plain view on the mantelpiece of his room. Their presence seemed suggestive and monitory in view of his emotional state. Even at the president's multiple entreaties for him to return to the White House, Randolph refused.

He was bled by physicians and became so weak he barely escaped death. Their advice to him was to quit politics and return to his family in Virginia. Eventually Randolph's mental state improved.

When Jefferson finished out his second term in 1809, he returned to Monticello, and at once brought Patsy and Randolph and their children under his own roof, along with the Eppes children.

Randolph quit politics and took up farming, at which he showed some talent. But because his father-in-law had taken over the financial obligations of his family, his self-esteem languished. He still flew into paroxysms of rage in front of his wife and children. And he was never able to save money. Instead, he gave it away to his own brothers and sisters who seemed always in debt and in need of help.

His daughter Ellen wrote of him: "As my father advanced in life, and his pecuniary difficulties increased, he became more morose, more irritable, more suspicious. My own belief is that nothing but the mingled dignity, forbearance and kindness of my grandfather prevented some outbreak which might forever have alienated two men bound by the strongest ties."

The person who took the most from Randolph was his oldest son, named after Thomas Jefferson. More than once Randolph tried to cane him, even when the boy grew to adulthood.

Jefferson, who spent his declining years as head of the household, continued to arbitrate the disputes, and suffered much of the emotional dissonance between Randolph and his family.

As he aged, Randolph once more entered politics, this time to run for governor of Virginia. He was elected three times: in 1819, 1820, and 1821. He spent two very successful years in the governor's chair, but when he tried to persuade Patsy to join him in Richmond, she refused. She claimed she was too busy taking care of her father and her children; in truth she was afraid of his rage and depression.

Randolph tried to keep straight, but he soon took to alcohol, and in his third year as governor he reverted to his old habits of quarreling publicly and making a fool of himself generally. Even his new friends soon forsook him.

Once again he became suicidal, writing in 1822 to his father-in-law: "I could flee to the grave with determined mind, to escape from such hateful sophistry and such unprincipled conduct and opinion as I have been compelled so long to witness and to hear."

His debts were escalating. When he left the governor's office, he owed $33,000. Sunken once again into his mental and physical depression, he decided to turn over the management of his affairs to his oldest boy, Thomas Jefferson.

He lived away from Monticello, and would speak neither to Jefferson nor to his own son. He refused to visit Monticello except at night. A friend described him at this point as "broke to atoms, in mind, body, and estate."

The financial mess was so bad his son Thomas Jefferson Randolph had to sell not only Edgehill, Randolph's own inheritance, but Varina as well. Randolph sank into total paranoia, accusing his father-in-law and his son of being in collusion with one another to ruin him and to plot against his welfare and his life.

"I am the victim of the avarice of one," he cried out to Jefferson, "encouraged . . . by the vengeance of many."

Jefferson begged his son-in-law to return to Monticello, but Randolph refused. The former president did not mention Randolph in his will at all, and ordered that he be refused control over any property left to Patsy.

When Jefferson died in 1828, Randolph took heart and found a job for himself, doing exploration and mapping along the Florida-Georgia border. When the job was finished, he had no more prospects and sank into alcoholism again. Finally he decided to come back to Monticello to start a new life with Patsy. However, he did not live with her and his children, but maintained residence in a separate part of the house.

Three months after his return he died, in June 1828, at the

age of sixty. Patsy lived eight years longer, dying at sixty-seven.

John and Abigail Adams's daughter had no better luck with her spouse than Jefferson's. Abigail Amelia, or "Nabby," was with her father and mother in London in 1785 when she met Colonel William Stephens Smith, then secretary of the United States legation.

The colonel was a good ten years older than Nabby, but he was an easygoing man who enjoyed the good life and who had been spoiled from birth by doting parents. Nabby was a demure girl, with a rather appealing vulnerability.

In fact, Nabby had just broken off an engagement to a Bostonian named Royall Tyler, who had seemed to her a bit slow in his pursuit of her, when she met Colonel Smith. The colonel was much more dashing, and his career in the army under General George Washington had given him some polish and spirit.

Both Nabby's parents approved of him. He was tactful, polite, and had a good "background." Also, he had at the time no noticeable vices, and, as Nabby's mother put it, was "of strict honor and unblemished reputation and morals, brave, modest and delicate."

Even the Bishop of St. Asaph who married them in 1786 assured the parents: "I have never married a couple with more pleasure because I never saw a fairer prospect of happiness."

How wrong he was.

The first child of the Smiths, William Steuben, Jr. was born in London, while the Adams family was still there. In 1788 Nabby and her husband moved to New York, where they lived with the Smiths out on Long Island. Nabby, brought up in a more stringent New England atmosphere, did not know what to do with the Smiths, who put on big-city airs and tended to patronize her.

Also, she found that her mother-in-law was overbearing

and tried to boss her around and take over the upbringing of Nabby's son. The family was a huge one, providing her with numerous brothers- and sisters-in-law.

Even the colonel diminished in stature in his home surroundings. Now he was simply a pampered and spoiled young son who rather liked to be adored and catered to without putting out any effort of his own. Someone who had appeared to be an aggressive realist in London now turned out to be a big-talking dreamer who formulated grandiose schemes for making his way in the world, usually involving real estate speculations, but who never seemed to get out and do an honest day's work.

Quite soon Nabby had another boy, this one named John after her father. Still the colonel did not have a job, but stayed around the house, basking in the adoration of his close family. When he went out, it was not to go to work, but rather to hunt with friends—he particularly loved to indulge himself shooting grouse on the Long Island flatlands—and visiting clubs and taverns.

In 1790 the colonel sailed for England—without Nabby—on a business venture he thought might help him strike it lucky and make a quick fortune. Nabby's mother, Abigail Adams, came to live with her and the children, who were now located near the Smiths in a smaller place. Nabby's brother Charles had moved in with them.

But Nabby was not particularly happy with her marital situation. According to her mother, she appeared "depressed." And she was beginning to put on weight; it made her look unhealthy. She worried about the colonel, away from home so much. And she fretted that he did not keep in touch by mail.

To the Adamses, each of whom overloaded every post with voluminous packets to one another, the colonel's actions were more than unforgivable; they were simply unimaginable.

The colonel returned from England, hoping to be appointed to live at the Court of St. James's to help settle disputed points of the Treaty of Paris. In London he had contacted Lord Grenville—Baron William Wyndham Grenville of the British Foreign Office and cousin of William Pitt—and Grenville thought him a perfect selection for the ministry. Smith went to the U.S. capital to plead his cause. But the appointment, when it came, went to another man.

Colonel Smith was not to be stopped. He immediately moved from politics to speculation and joined some well-to-do New Yorkers in a plan to merchandise American real estate to English investors.

He set out once again for England, and Nabby and the children went to Philadelphia to be with her parents. When the colonel returned from England, he plunged into his real estate ventures with renewed zeal, and made a killing with the sale of large portions of land.

For once the Smiths were rolling in money. Nabby even sailed to Europe with her husband, leaving the children in the care of the colonel's family. In Europe they were wined and dined by fashionable society, both in England and in France.

The colonel was a big spender from the word go. He flung his money everywhere he could, trying to impress rich Europeans. He dropped names wherever he was, mentioning his father-in-law's prestigious position in America, and making himself appear to be "in" with everyone who counted on both continents.

The French Revolution was in full swing. Nabby's father did not particularly sympathize with the peasants who had thrown out royalty. The colonel thought he could make his propositions look good to the new rich in France by cultivating the Jacobins; this aroused Adams's ire.

Though he decided that the colonel had "too little knowledge of the world; too little penetration; too little discretion," nevertheless, he thought him a "clever and agreeable" man. But he hated Smith's arrogant "boasting."

"Tell not of your prosperity," he advised his son-in-law,

"because it will make two men mad to one man glad; nor tell of your adversity, for it will make two men glad to one sad."

The colonel heard him out, and totally ignored his advice.

In 1794 Nabby had a daughter whom she named Caroline Amelia. The Smiths were then living on a grand scale. The colonel could now indulge in as much ostentation and spending as he pleased. The life-style of the Smiths went totally against the grain of the Adamses: balls, dinners, assemblies, and hunting on Long Island.

The animosity between the colonel and his father-in-law grew. Adams could not stomach boasting and arrogance. But he bit his tongue and did not give vent to his feelings.

Within a few months, the Smiths' great and good fortune popped like a soap bubble. Among the many European businessmen with whom the colonel dealt was one smooth-talking French financier who was as much a liar and cheat as he was a hail-fellow-well-met.

He managed to con the glib and boastful, but not very bright, Yankee colonel out of a great sum of money. The speculation in which the colonel involved himself wound up a total disaster. The "swindler and mountebank" got away with every last cent the colonel had.

The result was that Colonel Smith was forced to declare bankruptcy. When the vice-president heard the fate of his son-in-law, he was honestly outraged and even a bit sympathetic:

"It is the decree of fate that I should be connected by two branches with a weak family and I must make the best of it. Nothing can happen from it worse than my fears and long expectations."

The fact was, as one biographer expressed it, Nabby was simply married to a man who was nothing more than a "pretentious simpleton."

The free-handed Smith life-style collapsed with the colonel's bankruptcy. But when John Adams was elected president in 1797, the colonel's fortunes picked up. It was Adams's desire to appoint his son-in-law adjutant general, a high post in the army. However, three members of Congress in his own party asked him to withdraw Smith's name, calling him "a speculator . . . a bankrupt, and an Anti-Federalist."

Adams refused to take his son-in-law's name from the list. However, when the list came up for Senate approval, the Senate dropped him.

In telling his son-in-law that he had tried to push through his appointment as adjutant general, Adams could not refrain from letting him know how he really felt about him.

"Upon this occasion I must be plain with you. Your pride and ostentation, which I myself have seen with inexpressible grief for many years, have excited among your neighbors so much envy and resentment, that if they have to allege against you any instance of dishonorable and dishonest conduct, as it is pretended they have, you may depend upon it, it will never be forgiven or forgotten. . . . It is a great misfortune to the public that the office I hold should be disgraced by a nomination of my son-in-law, which the Senate of the United States think themselves obliged to negative."

To his wife, the First Lady, then in Boston, the president wrote: "All the actions of my life and all the conduct of my children have not yet disgraced me so much as this man. His pay will not feed his dogs; and his dogs must be fed if his children starve. What a folly!"

The president then recommended the colonel for a commission as lieutenant colonel in command of a provisional regiment that was being formed to prepare for imminent war. In spite of the secretary of war's opposition, the Senate passed Smith's appointment.

Privately the president hoped that Smith would refuse the command, since it was a rank below that which he had won during the Revolution, but the colonel took it anyway.

For some months Smith was busy organizing his regiment; he seemed in his element and happy. However, his happiness was to be short-lived. Political vicissitudes caused the War

Department to disband the regiment, and he was once again out of a job. Smith swallowed his pride and begged the president for another commission. Adams discussed commissioning Smith in the regular army as a brigadier general with Alexander Hamilton, but Hamilton advised against it, pointing out that he was too close in relationship to the president to avoid the charge of nepotism.

When Adams was defeated in his bid for reelection, one of his last acts was the nomination of his son-in-law to be surveyor of the district of New York and inspector of the revenue. It took the Senate three months to give its reluctant consent to the appointment.

The post was a lucrative one and a soft touch indeed. But in the sinecure Colonel Smith seemed to chaff against the very ease at which he collected his salary. There was not enough excitement, not enough adventure, not enough glitter about the work. So the colonel decided to moonlight.

His opportunity came when he was approached by a Spanish mercenary, Francisco Miranda. Miranda was a friend of Napoleon's, and, like the colonel, a dashing and half-crazy romantic.

He had a long history of revolutionary activity. Born in Caracas, Venezuela, he became an army officer and eventually served with the French during the Revolution. The success of the Revolution convinced him that he could secure independence for Venezuela from Spain. After living in many European countries, he came to America to seek help in trying to throw off the yoke of Spanish tyranny.

All well and good—but how?

Colonel Smith was an old hand at military ventures. When Miranda outlined his hopes to Smith, the colonel rubbed his hands in glee. He immediately began raising money from his affluent friends, and with the particular help of S. G. Ogden, he put together a landing party that could be transported to Venezuela for overthrow of the government.

The revolutionists outfitted the warship *Leander* in 1806. Colonel Smith continued to put together the landing force.

His oldest son, William Steuben Smith, was now attending Columbia College. Like his father, he was a sturdy, soldierly type even in his teens. The excitement of a real military adventure seized him—particularly since his father was building it up as such a tremendous challenge—and he became a lieutenant to Miranda himself. And dropped out of Columbia College to do the job.

The *Leander* set sail.

At home, John Adams was in turmoil. The worst of it was that his grandson had dropped out of college to pursue some military will-o'-the-wisp. "I saw the ruin of my only daughter and her goodhearted enthusiastic husband," he wrote, "and I had no other hope or prayer than that the ship with my grandson in it might be sunk in the Gulf Stream!"

No such luck. Miranda joined forces with a British admiral named Sir A. Cochrane. The British were momentarily engaged in war with both France and Spain. The marine force made a successful landing near Caracas. Miranda proclaimed the country's freedom.

A sudden vicissitude in international politics caused the British to withdraw from the invasion, leaving the American recruits at the mercy of the Venezuelan regulars. The Yankee force was captured almost in its entirety, and the mercenaries were put in irons and hauled away to prison to await trial for insurrection.

Adams refused to intercede with the Spanish ambassador, the Marquis d'Yrujo, in an effort to have his grandson released. Tight-lipped, Adams vowed that his grandson must share the fate of all his doomed and indiscreet companions.

"New York has been the box of Pandora to me and my family," Adams lamented. "I do not complain," he went on, belying his statement. "It is enough for me to suffer in my own heart and never torment others with endeavors to excite their compassion. I have no reason to hope that my name will contribute in the smallest degree to save the life of my grandson."

Nor did he have much sympathy for Colonel Smith. When

the news of the abortive landing made the headlines, Smith was summarily dismissed from his sinecure as surveyor of the District of New York by President Thomas Jefferson, who didn't like Adams *or* Smith.

When news of Smith's dismissal came to Adams, he huffed: "That absurdity of his conduct through the whole business cannot be too severely reprobated."

Eventually the boy was freed and returned home, chastened and humiliated. But the colonel's fate was a harsher one. Fed up with his own insufficiency and blaming his own inability to land with both feet on the ground on bad luck, he moved himself and his family to the western portion of New York State, where he once again began dabbling in real estate ventures.

Within three years, Nabby was ill with cancer. She died a year later.

The colonel lived some time longer. After spending several disastrous years in his land speculations, he returned to New York and ran for Congress. To the surprise of everyone he was elected in 1813, and moved to Washington. Three years later, early in 1816, he died in New York, with his daughter Caroline at his bedside.

"Be to his virtues ever kind, to his faults a little blind," Adams wrote to his own son, John Quincy Adams, the colonel's brother-in-law. "The world will never know all the good or all the evil he has done."

12

Heroin, Homicide, and Horror

At about 5:30 P.M. on September 5, 1979, an individual known in the Harlem area of the Shelton Plaza Hotel at 300 West 116th Street as White James drew his BMW sports coupe up to the curb near Eighth Avenue.

Two men on the sidewalk, White James said later, had "signaled" him to join them. White James parked the car and got out. There was a short conversation. White James walked into the lobby of the Shelton Hotel, which was only a few steps away.

Then, White James said, the two men from the sidewalk tried to beat him up and rob him of the two hundred dollars he carried with him. According to his story, they dragged him onto a stairway at the back of the lobby and punched him and slammed him against the wall. He began to bleed; he had bruises that he later said had been sustained in the attack. The men got only thirty dollars of his two hundred.

Meanwhile some interested bystanders decided that White James was in trouble. One of them saw him being beaten up inside the Shelton. Someone called 911 and said that a white man was being mugged in the lobby of the hotel. One version of the story had it that White James had not been alone in the car, but was accompanied by an unidentified person who later made the 911 call.

Members of the Twenty-eighth Precinct of the New York Police Department had known for some time what the Shelton was used for: It was reputed to be a place where drugs could be bought and used.

Within minutes a patrol car skidded to a stop, its siren blaring. The noise and flashing lights tipped off the muggers who fled into the hotel's shadowy interior. White James lay bleeding in the corner. Two police officers dragged him out into the street.

Immediately the place was swarming with cops—in plainclothes and uniforms. A room on the third floor of the hotel was searched, leading to the discovery of twenty-five decks of heroin. Traces of the muggers were found in the room. Apparently they had escaped from the hotel via the fire escape or some other means of exit.

One man was caught and brought down to be confronted by White James; he was immediately released when the victim assured the police that he was not one of the men who had beaten him up.

Now the police discovered that White James was simply a sobriquet used by Harlem pushers and habitues of the hotel. White James was actually David Anthony Kennedy, the son of the late Robert F. Kennedy and the nephew of the late John F. Kennedy, once the thirty-fifth president of the United States.

At one point David was said to have admitted that he was attempting to buy heroin at the hotel.

"I'm a stoned-out junkie," he reportedly said. The quotation later appeared in a national magazine.

But at the time, none of the details were released to the

press. The members of the police department knew the magic of the Kennedy name. They were careful not to let out too many facts so as not to offend the Kennedy family or friends of the Kennedys.

"Police here know you don't mess around with Kennedys," one person was quoted as saying.

David Anthony Kennedy was not put under arrest at all, in spite of the fact that he had apparently admitted he was trying to purchase heroin. He was sent home.

Police immediately began combing the area to see if anyone else knew where the muggers were. It was then discovered that Kennedy had made frequent appearances at the Shelton in the recent past. His nickname, White James, had been given him because he had first been introduced to contacts at the Shelton by a black man named James.

"They got so many Jameses up here they put the tag 'White James' on Kennedy to differentiate him from all the other Jameses," one informant said.

In spite of the surreptitious nature of the police investigations, news of Kennedy's mugging leaked out. Within minutes there were police reporters all over the place. The reporters immediately found out that David was a frequenter of the area.

"I've seen him before, a few times in the past months," one man told a *New York Daily News* reporter. "You can't believe what the cops say, that he came down here and just parked and followed the two guys into here."

Meanwhile David had arrived at his apartment on 72nd Street, had packed his bags, had thrown them in his car, and had headed, as all Kennedys did when they were in trouble, to Hyannis Port, on Cape Cod.

There he was put to bed and placed under medication.

This was not by any means David Anthony Kennedy's first scrape with the law. When he was twelve, he and a nearby neighbor in McLean, Virginia, had been arrested for throwing rocks at a passing car.

That had been in 1968, when his father was the junior senator from New York in Washington. The senator's office had issued a statement:

"I regret to say that one of my sons in the company of another boy got into trouble . . . while my wife and I were away from home. He feels very badly about what he has done and has apologized to all concerned. He is a good boy . . . and never has been involved in any trouble whatsoever prior to this incident."

Shortly after that David hid a cherry bomb in a mailbox of a nearby house in McLean. No statement came from the senator's office when the story of that escapade was published.

Five years later David was involved as a passenger in a serious automobile accident. The driver of the car was his older brother Joseph Patrick Kennedy III.

Joe was in trouble himself at the time. He had dropped out of the University of California at Berkeley, had quit a job in San Francisco, and had suffered an automobile accident in California. Having moved to Nantucket, he and his brother David had taken a number of girls to the beach one day at Siasconset in a Toyota jeep borrowed from a friend.

The car, crowded with seven bathers, including Joe and David, swerved to avoid an oncoming car, and flipped over onto the verge of the road and smashed into a tree. The car was demolished.

Joe was unhurt. Of the five girls driving with them, one was paralyzed for life from the waist down, another sustained a fractured pelvis and would limp for life, and the three other girls were hurt in various ways.

David sustained a serious back injury, spent a great deal of time under medical treatment, and was in excruciating pain for weeks. He was given medication to alleviate the pain. The drugs were narcotics, the first he had ever taken; one of them was Percodan, a powerful painkiller. Even after he had been transferred from the hospital to his home, he continued on the prescribed tranquilizers.

Later on, the pain seemed to return. In addition to Percodan, David was given Dilauded. But he was suffering from more than physical injuries. His problems were psychological as well as physical, and for them he was given Quaaludes.

Death had become an obsession with him.

When he was eight years old, his uncle Jack—President John F. Kennedy—had been murdered by an assassin in Dallas.

When he was twelve years old, his father—Senator Robert F. Kennedy—had been murdered by an assassin in Los Angeles.

And now, when he was eighteen years old, he himself had almost been killed in an automobile accident.

It was not the first time he had eluded sudden death. On the very day his own father was murdered, David himself had escaped death by an eyelash.

It was June 5, 1968. He was swimming at Malibu Beach in California at the house of one of his father's political supporters. It was a foggy day, but most of the mist had burned off by early afternoon. Now, however, the tide had changed perceptibly.

David was body-surfing, catching waves, and riding them in to shore. Suddenly he found himself out of his depth; an undertow was pulling him out to sea.

"Help me!" he screamed. "I can't stand up!"

His father plunged in and rescued him.

He tried not to show it—it was a Kennedy trait to not show fear or cry—but David was frightened. He knew he had come within an ace of drowning in that unpredictable and strong rip tide. But he kept the knowledge inside him.

That same night, long after he should have been asleep, he was watching television in the Ambassador Hotel, where his father was celebrating his primary victory in California, and learned that his father had been shot to death by an assassin—just like his Uncle Jack.

Again he kept it all in. But a strange thought may have occurred to him. Was there not the possibility that his own life had been traded for his father's? Perhaps because his dad had cheated death by rescuing him, death had taken his father in retribution.

Quite probably David never thought of it that way, but his psyche may have. And he might have assumed guilt for his father's assassination. When he once again had cheated death in his brother Joe's car in 1973, he may have known he was living on borrowed time.

Then in 1975, just after his twentieth birthday, David was arrested for speeding in his own Toyota near New Market, Virginia.

More guilt. More worry. Meanwhile, David's career at Harvard was not progressing as smoothly as it should. He was trying hard, but he did not seem able to make good grades. He finished his sophomore year, not without some trouble, and then started his junior year.

Brushes with the law continued.

He ran a stop sign and was again stopped by the police. This time he was driving without a license. This contempt for the law, both in disregarding speed laws *and* in not being properly licensed, was only a symptom of more submerged psychological problems.

Friends began to notice that David would be subject to frequent depressions.

Then, quite abruptly, in March 1976, he was in Massachusetts General Hospital, suffering from pneumonia. But it was the cause of the pneumonia that troubled his family. He was suffering from an inflammation of the lymph glands, a symptom that might be caused by the shooting of drugs.

David's mind began to drift. He became vague. He didn't seem able to recognize the difference between reality and fantasy. In February 1977, he was speeding again, and ordered to court in Arlington, Massachusetts. He was driving a car that was unregistered and uninsured—and driving it without a license.

A year later, in April 1978, he was in Mass General—again with pneumonia. He was put in the intensive care unit, under the charge of Dr. Lee Macht, a prominent Harvard psychiatry professor and chief of psychiatry at Cambridge City Hospital. Macht prescribed various tranquilizers for him: Percodan, Dialuded, and Quaaludes.

David dropped out of Harvard and moved to New York, where he rented an apartment on East 72nd Street. He hit the discos, some of which were alleged to be drops where various hard drugs could be procured. He seemed to have straightened out after a year of living in New York and enrolled at Boston College. But after only a few months he dropped out again and began hanging around with friends here and there.

Meanwhile, authorities were investigating illegal drug prescriptions in Middlesex County; David's psychiatrist, Dr. Lee Macht, was one of the targets of the investigation.

David was twenty-four years old now, and drifting dangerously. He was unable to find himself or to help himself. When he tried to get pill prescriptions from his psychiatrist, he found he couldn't. The drug culture was in the midst of a periodic shutdown. Addicts were in trouble. So was David. Bruised and beaten in Harlem.

David didn't stay long in Hyannis Port after his release by the police following the Harlem incident. On the following Monday he escaped the Kennedy compound and was finally located the next day by the authorities.

At that point, the Kennedys had had enough. They issued a statement and took over the problem themselves.

"David turned himself over to the family and he will be receiving long-term 'treatment' for his drug habit," a statement said.

And that was all.

"I'm a stoned-out junkie," White James had told the police. The Kennedy family knew David's psychiatrist, Dr. Macht, was not available for help. After pleading not guilty to charges of prescribing drugs without notifying the state mental health department, he paid a $1,000 fine and had his drug license lifted for a year.

David was sent to Sacramento, California, where he was put into the charge of Donald Juhl, the former executive director of a California drug-abuse program called Aquarian Effort.

In July 1980, David made the newspapers again when he was arrested for driving in a state of intoxication, going the wrong way down a one-way street in downtown Sacramento. When the arresting officers gave him the sobriety test, he flunked it. He was booked for driving without a license—again—and then released in his own custody.

Juhl was quoted in the newspaper stories about the episode to the effect that David's difficulties with the police this time had nothing to do with his drug-abuse problem. "They're all over," Juhl said, referring to David's drug addiction. "He's in no trouble."

Thomas Jefferson was always being haunted by relatives. In 1792, some years before Jefferson became president, a close kin—Anne Cary Randolph, sister-in-law and cousin to Jefferson's daughter Martha Randolph—was involved in a bizarre case of homicide, along with her lover and cousin, Richard Randolph.

Relationships within the Jefferson family were complicated, involving many intermarriages between cousins. Working out from the Thomas Jefferson family, the genealogy went this way:

Martha, Jefferson's eldest daughter, who was called Patsy, was married to Thomas Mann Randolph, Jr., a cousin on Jefferson's mother's side. Anne Cary Randolph was one of Thomas's sisters. She was always called Nancy to distinguish her from her mother, the original Anne Cary Randolph.

The Randolph line from which Thomas Mann and Anne Cary came was called the Tuckahoe line, after their home estate.

Another of Thomas Mann Randolph, Jr.'s sisters, Judith, was married to her cousin Richard Randolph, known as Richard Randolph of Bizarre, the name of that Randolph line, after their family estate.

Bizarre was not, in the words of one visitor, "bizarre at all" in appearance; it was the name of an earlier manor house that *was* bizarre in every detail. The Randolphs' Bizarre was a reconstructed mansion built on the site of the old one.

If the place wasn't bizarre in appearance, a miasma of alcoholism, lust, and madness seemed to hang over it like a cloud. On her marriage to Richard of Bizarre, Judith Randolph Randolph moved there to live.

Richard had two brothers, Theodorick, one year younger, and John, three years younger.

Getting back to Anne Cary Randolph—Nancy—she became engaged to Theodorick, Richard's brother, in 1791. She was sixteen; he was twenty.

But Nancy's father, Thomas Mann Randolph, Sr., opposed the match, even though he had championed the marriage between his daughter Judith and Richard. Theodorick was a sick man; he suffered from "consumption," a popular term for tuberculosis. He was a "mere skeleton," hardly able to walk. "His bones," one observer said, "were worn through his skin."

He died early in 1792. Nancy was visiting her sister Judith at the time, staying at Bizarre, preparatory to marrying Theodorick. Judith was pregnant, and in May 1792, delivered a baby named St. George Randolph, after a favorite uncle. The baby turned out to be deaf.

During and after the childbirth, Judith was in ill health. One story said that she was treated for recurring pain and postpartum depression with opium; in the process she became addicted to the drug. But even if that story was untrue, it was obvious that the birth was not a happy one for anyone concerned.

What happened afterward is not truly known to this day. But by piecing together information supplied at the sensational trial that occurred in 1793, it is assumed that Judith's husband, Richard, turned to Judith's sister, Nancy, for solace during those trying days at Bizarre.

The death of his younger brother, followed by the birth of a handicapped child, followed by the long illness of his wife, were just too much for him. He and Nancy apparently became involved in a love affair. During the course of the liaison, Nancy became pregnant.

At least that is the story told by her aunt, Polly Cary Page—who peeked through a slightly ajar bedroom door to see Nancy stripped naked and seemingly pregnant. Later on, Aunt Polly was chatting with Nancy's sister-in-law Patsy Jefferson Randolph and in the course of the conversation discussed "gum guaiacum"—a "good medicine" for certain ailments, but bad because it induced abortion.

Nancy apparently overheard the conversation. No one ever knew what *really* happened, but strange rumors began circulating among the Randolph slaves some months thereafter. The story was a gruesome one: Someone had found a fetus, or the remains of a new-born child, in a pile of debris out near the slave quarters.

It was easy enough to construct a damning story by putting together a few random facts. Thus: Richard and Nancy had indulged in an incestuous love affair; had produced a child; had destroyed the child either before or during childbirth; and had tried to hide the remains. It was thought that the abortifacient gum guaiacum may have been used to terminate the pregnancy.

The story that emerged became common currency in Virginia.

In April 1793, Richard Randolph was arrested and held in jail without bond on a charge of infanticide. Although Nancy was apparently not jailed, she was charged with complicity. Both were remanded for trial on a charge of felonious homicide.

Patsy Jefferson, Richard's sister-in-law, was asked to testify at the trial as a character witness for Nancy. Patrick Henry (of "Give me liberty or give me death!" fame) was persuaded to act as counsel for the defense. He was offered 250 guineas at first, but the aging and mercenary attorney managed to elevate the fee to 500. John Marshall, later chief justice of the United States, became his cocounsel for the defense. A third lawyer, Alexander Campbell, famous locally, joined these stellar attractions. The trial became the sensation of its day, played before a distinguished jury of sixteen and as many Virginians as could crowd into the bulging courthouse.

The story reeked of decadence: incest, infanticide, lust, drugs, poison. There were descriptions of Nancy's screams and moans—was it during childbirth? There was Aunt Polly's story of spying on Nancy through a crack in a door.

Patrick Henry, a consummate actor even in his dotage, leaped to his feet at this point, exclaiming dramatically:

"Madame! Which eye did you peep with?"

His histrionics brought down the house.

But, of course, there was no evidence. The existence of the fetus was never established. And even an eyewitness account of it could not be given, because slaves, under the law, could not testify in court. Besides, even assuming the fetus did exist, was Richard necessarily the father? Could not the "child," if Nancy's, have been Theodorick's?

The jury brought in a verdict of not guilty. There were loud cheers and rejoicing in the courtroom.

Although he had won the case, Marshall did not know for sure whether his clients were guilty or innocent.

"The friends of Miss Randolph," he decided, "cannot deny that there is some foundation on which suspicion may build; nor can it be denied by [Nancy's] enemies but that every circumstance may be accounted for without imputing guilt to her. In this situation, candor will not condemn, or exclude from society, a person who may be only unfortunate."

As for Thomas Jefferson's daughter, Patsy believed Nancy innocent, and Richard not:

"As for the poor deluded victim," she wrote her father, "I believe all feel much more for her than she does for herself. The villain having been no less successful in corrupting her mind than he has in destroying her reputation. Amidst the distress of her family she alone is tranquil and seems proof against every other misfortune on earth but that of a separation from her vile seducer."

Following the trial Nancy continued to live at Bizarre with her sister and brother-in-law. Richard's state of mind after the trial was one of relief to a degree, but anxiety and concern about his own future. He had been put through a crucible of torment. He felt exhausted and undone. Now the household at Bizarre became the scene of recriminations and endless bickering.

John Randolph, the third brother of the Bizarre Randolphs, had once been in love with Nancy, before she had become engaged to Theodorick. John was typically Randolph—a mixture of talent and recklessness, tempered with sloth and lust. He had been serious about Nancy, but she had rejected him outright. He still smarted from that humiliation. In his own mind he was quite sure that Nancy had led Richard on; quite sure that she had indeed murdered her own infant.

In John's words later, there were quarrels between Nancy and Judith, "before fierce and angry," but now with "no remission." John saw Judith as the victim, with Nancy the victimizer. Apparently the two sisters did quarrel, but apparently the affair between Nancy and Richard, if it had ever existed, ceased to do so.

New events occurred which led John to suspect Nancy of consorting with one of the Randolph slaves, a man named Billy Ellis. In a fiery confrontation, he one day accused Nancy of fornication with that certain "Othello," and asked her in the presence of his sister:

"Nancy, when do you leave this house? The sooner the better for you to take as much liberties as if you were in a tavern!"

And Nancy replied: "I will go as soon as I can." And she ran out of the room in tears. But she did not move from Bizarre. She stayed.

Four years from the time of the trial, Richard Randolph caught a "fever" of some undetermined origin, and failed to rally. His own guilt—or his riddled self-esteem—may have sapped his strength to a dangerous degree. He died early in 1796. Judith had just given birth to a second son, Theodorick Tudor Randolph.

In the tormented mind of John Randolph, still animated against Nancy, the seeds of new doubts began to sprout. Did his brother Richard die of fever—or was he poisoned? Soon the outlines of a lurid plot began to take shape in his mind. Its villainess was Nancy; its victim his brother Richard. Or was it Judith who was the villainess? Either could have slipped some kind of poison into Richard's food.

Soon John was accusing Nancy to her face of murdering his brother. The house was in constant turmoil. Nancy tired of being accused of so many crimes and indiscretions, and left Bizarre for good. She sought residence in various places in Virginia, becoming a kind of vagrant.

Meanwhile, John was faring little better. He had become incapacitated by a bad case of scarlet fever; it was said he had been left impotent by its inroads. Rumors of his ailment went the rounds of Virginia; he was rejected by several women to whom he proposed.

He began collecting facts about Nancy—that she was living in a public house and was no more than a common prostitute; that she was trying to entice rich widowers to marry her; and so on.

Then began a series of letters between the two of them in which John once again accused Nancy of murdering his brother, of fornication with a slave, and of prostitution, and in which she accused him of jealousy and vindictiveness. John never made any formal accusations, but everyone knew about the charges and denials because the two scribes circulated their letters about among their friends.

In 1809 Nancy was acting as housekeeper for a fifty-six-year-old philanderer, broken-down aristocrat, and so-called American statesman named Gouverneur Morris. Morris had been minister to France during the Revolution, and had participated in a daring and unsuccessful plot to smuggle the king and queen of France out of the country during the blood bath. He had also received enormous emoluments of jewels and silver from other members of the fleeing nobility. Now he was an aging libertine with a pegleg and an eye for the ladies.

When he asked Nancy to marry him, she accepted. "I glory in stating that I was married in a gown patched at the elbows," she wrote to anyone who wanted to read.

John Randolph kept up his barrage of insults and accusations through the next several years. By now he had left Bizarre and established himself in Roanoke, calling himself John Randolph of Roanoke, as if Bizarre was something out of a bad dream.

In point of fact, Bizarre ceased to exist at about this time, burning to the ground in 1813. Nancy and her husband tried to help Judith and the children in every way they could.

To his death John continued to tell the world that Nancy had killed his brother. To her death Nancy continued to deny it.

Who was right?

Less than three years after Jefferson had retired from the presidency two of his nephews, Lilburn and Isham Lewis, sons of Jefferson's sister Lucy Jefferson Lewis, became involved in an odious incident that had more resemblance to a half-mad Grand Guignol drama than to real life in Virginia.

The Lewis brothers were unsavory backwoods planters who operated land in nearby Kentucky. Both were heavy drinkers and reprehensible individuals who did not have much good standing in the community.

Because of their muscular physiques and surly, ingrown natures, they were extremely hard to deal with. They were particularly rough on their slaves. They would beat them and curse them and drive them mercilessly, especially when they were drunk on rotgut whiskey they always had at hand.

Most of their blacks hated them in return. There was little chance for any of them to escape; the social status quo of the time allowed a white master unlimited privileges in dealing with the slaves he owned. Nevertheless, the Lewises suffered several losses by runaways and decided to make an example of the next fugitive returned.

A teenaged black owned by the Lewises ran away after a beating, only to be caught by white neighbors. He was returned to the Lewises even though he pleaded for mercy and said anything would be better than to go back home.

The Lewises assembled all their slaves in the plantation meathouse. And there, right before their eyes, they knifed the seventeen-year-old runaway to death. They then dismembered his body, using butcher knives, throwing the arms and legs one by one into a burning stove in the corner of the meat house.

The blacks were too frightened to tell the authorities. But soon the news leaked out, as it was bound to. Neighbors searched the premises when the Lewises were out carousing and discovered the bones of the slain youth in the meat house.

Now the neighborhood was aroused. Nobody liked the Lewises anyway. A white lynch mob formed, this one organized to hunt down whites rather than blacks.

Meanwhile the law took a hand. After all, the Lewises were related to the former president of the United States—and closely at that.

Hasty indictments were drawn up for the two brothers. They were arrested, protected from the wrath of the mob, and tried for murder in another sensational trial.

Both were sentenced to life imprisonment.

Eventually, Lilburn Lewis killed himself in prison. It was said to be an accident. Nothing about Lilburn's fate is clear at this distance today.

Isham Lewis somehow escaped from prison. He was almost immediately apprehended and sentenced to hang. It was believed that he had been allowed to escape into the hands of waiting authorities so he could be put to the rope.

However, he escaped once again. From that moment on he vanished from sight. It was said that he eventually worked his way down to New Orleans, where he died in the Battle of New Orleans.

The former president never said a word about the crime, nor was any notice of it ever found in his papers or letters. The Lewises were, unfortunately, very close kinfolk to the third president of the United States.

920
Pre

920 Pre

DATE DUE

AUTHOR
Adler, Bill
TITLE
All in the First Family with the Presidents
DATE DUE | BORROWER'S NAME

920
Pre

HARTFORD PUBLIC LIBRARY